GUIDE TO LOCAL AND FAMILY HISTORY AT THE NEWBERRY LIBRARY

By Peggy Tuck Sinko

Ancestry Publishing

P.O. Box 476
Salt Lake City, UT 84110

Library of Congress Catalog Card Number 87-70110
ISBN Number 0-916489-24-8 (Hardbound)

First Printing 1987
10 9 8 7 6 5 4 3 2 1

Printed in the United States of America.

CONTENTS

PREFACE

The Newberry Library has long been recognized as one of the country's leading institutions for the study of local and family history. During my years on the staff of the Local and Family History Section, 1974-83, I came to recognize the need for an in-depth guide that would alert interested researchers to the great storehouse of material available at the Newberry. Various information bulletins and the Newberry's *Genealogy Beginners' Manual* only scratched the surface. In 1983 I was able to begin work on this project. My goal was to prepare a work that would give Newberry Library patrons and potential patrons a sense of the scope, strengths, and weaknesses of the collection and alert them to unique, unusual, or overlooked sources. While genealogists are the primary audience for this guide, it is not designed solely for their use. Local historians, librarians, scholars, and others will, I hope, also find this guide beneficial.

The first task was to determine what form the guide would take. The formats of numerous catalogues, guides, and bibliographies seemed unsatisfactory for this project. A bibliographic listing of each item in the Local and Family History collection would have been overwhelming and not the best means by which to introduce researchers to the collection. I finally decided to organize my discussion of the holdings into three categories: special subjects, special Newberry Library sources, and geographical areas. Each chapter is partly descriptive, partly bibliographic.

Any work of this kind will of necessity be highly subjective, and this guide does reflect my knowledge, interests, and eccentricities. I am in no way an expert on every topic covered and have depended on the advice and expertise of numerous individuals. Nonetheless, I am sure to have overlooked significant sources and to have included some insignificant ones, and I take full responsibility for decisions to include, exclude, or emphasize particular material.

My work on the guide has been sometimes tedious, often excruciatingly slow, but always interesting and educational. I was continually amazed and delighted to discover material about which I had no previous knowledge, and my respect for the incredible scope and variety of the Newberry collections has increased accordingly. This great library truly is "an uncommon collection of uncommon collections."

Many people have helped make this guide possible. I would like to thank first and foremost the staff of The Newberry Library for their interest, encouragement, and assistance. David Thackery, Curator of Local and Family History, and Rita Fitzgerald both read the entire manuscript and have my heartfelt thanks. David kept me apprised of new acquisitions and developments, while Rita kept many of my most outrageous sentences from reaching the printed page. Other library staff members have been most generous with their assistance: Cynthia H. Peters and her staff in the Reference and Bibliographical Center; John Aubrey, Diana Haskell, and Robert W. Karrow of Special Collections; the General Reading Room and Technical Services staffs; and Richard Seidel and Mary P. Wyly. Brian Donovan, Mary Powell Hammersmith, Sandra Hargreaves Luebking, Ronald Otto, and Elizabeth Pearson White all have my thanks for reading and commenting on portions of the manuscript. Michele Piotrowski, who provided loving care for my son, helped me find the time and gave me the peace of mind I needed for this project. I would like especially to thank my sister, Susan K. Bellile, for the use of her computer and for her technical assistance. Finally, my deepest thanks goes to my husband Kenn and son Andrew who helped in so many important ways. Their support, encouragement, and occasional prodding were instrumental in making this book a reality.

Oak Park, Illinois
January, 1987

INTRODUCTION

This guide to the local and family history holdings of The Newberry Library is divided into three parts: special subjects, special Newberry Library sources, and geographical areas. These divisions seemed to reflect best the questions most frequently asked about the library's holdings. Users of the guide should first consult the Table of Contents and then the Index. A search of the Index is essential to be sure that all references to a particular topic have been located. Researchers interested in individual states should also read the appropriate introductory regional chapter.

Some explanation of the guide's contents is necessary:

1. The guide is not limited to material under the jurisdiction of the Local and Family History Section. Material from all parts of the Library--Special Collections, Maps, Modern Manuscripts, General Collections--has been included when it relates to local and family history.

2. The guide concentrates on those works available at The Newberry Library. Bibliographies and catalogues of other library collections are included when they are useful in identifying works also at the Newberry. Guides to manuscript or archival collections at other institutions have been omitted, although the Newberry has an outstanding collection of these. Also excluded from the bibliographic listings are newspaper bibliographies and guides to early state imprints, including the American Imprints Inventories. Again, the Library has excellent holdings of these.

3. The guide omits most references to works on American Indians that are not of genealogical value.

4. The Newberry's local history holdings are quite extensive, although the Library does not (with a few exceptions) actively collect works that are primarily pictorial; textbooks; very general, popular ac-

counts; and most pamphlets under 100 pages.

5.   Generally speaking, the Library does not collect Master's theses or Ph.D dissertations. For a time in the 1960s and 1970s some dissertations in local and family history were acquired, but the overall number is small.

6.   When dates are given for periodical or serial publications,   the beginning date is volume 1, unless otherwise indicated.

7.   Throughout the guide the term "genealogical source material" is used. This is my shorthand for those compilations containing the basic names,   dates,   and   family   relationship   information   sought   by genealogists.   These   include   records   of   births,   deaths,   marriages, probates, cemeteries, deeds, taxes, court records, Bible records, etc.

8.   The bibliographies concluding most chapters are highly   selective. Works are included which I believe are the most important, basic, or useful titles to introduce researchers to the literature.   Marginal works are only included when nothing better is available. The list of periodicals for each state and country is again selective. A title is included if the Library has a substantial run of the periodical, or if it is considered important despite its brief life. I have attempted to include all local and family history journals with state-wide coverage.

9.   In order to give researchers some sense of the scope and quality of the Library's holdings, I have chosen to use highly subjective terms such as "poor," "fair," "good," or "excellent." Although some may quarrel with the use of such labels, I felt that some indication of the collection's strengths and weaknesses in each area is useful. The label for a particular topic was based on my own personal knowledge   of the topic, the knowledge of others familiar with the Newberry collection, and in many cases a check of the library's holdings against standard bibliographies. "Some" or "fair" means that a few basic works are available. Researchers could obtain general knowledge of a subject, but do little in-depth research. "Good" means most standard   works, as well as many works of a secondary or collateral importance are available. "Very good" means all standard works, as well as a large number of secondary or collateral works are available. "Excellent," "outstanding," and "strong" are reserved for those holdings where the material is of such abundance and significance that extensive, in-depth, detailed research is possible.

CHAPTER 1

HINTS FOR LOCATING MATERIAL AT THE NEWBERRY LIBRARY

The Newberry Library is a closed stack library, and patrons must use the card catalogues to locate and identify material of interest. Due to the size of the Library's collection (over 1 million volumes), patrons are sometimes intimidated by the size and number of catalogues and are often uncertain of how to proceed.

There are several different card catalogues, all located in the Reference and Bibliographical Center. More than one catalogue must often be searched in order to be sure of locating all material of interest. The Card Catalogue, which contains cards for all printed books in the library's general and special collections, is in two parts. Each is a dictionary catalogue; that is, author, title and subject cards are all filed together in one alphabet. The larger of the two catalogues includes all books acquired by the library through 1980. To comply with changes made nationally in the rules governing the cataloguing and description of books, the Newberry began a new card catalogue for all books acquired after 1980. If, therefore, a book printed in 1793 was acquired by the Library in 1982, that book, despite its date of publication, will appear in the New Card Catalogue. In the very near future patrons will also find computer terminals in the Reference and Bibliographical Center. All post-1980 acquisitions, as well as some selected earlier acquisitions, will become part of an online public catalogue.

Other card catalogues of interest to local and family history researchers include the Map Catalogue, Modern Manuscripts Catalogue,

Shelflist, Local and Family History Vertical File, City Directory File, and Chicago and Cook County Biography and Industry File. All of these are located in the Reference and Bibliographical Center. Most are described in greater detail elsewhere in this guide.

The best advice I can give researchers as they approach the catalogues is to think creatively and not to be afraid to ask for help. Because the Card Catalogue is so massive, and is a dictionary catalogue, researchers often get bogged down and never find what they need. For example, if one is seeking information on Washington County, Pennsylvania, one will be confronted with a large number of catalogue cards on various people, places, and things called Washington; cards for works by and about people named Washington; title cards and subject cards on various counties and cities named Washington; Washington, D. C.; Washington State; and so on.

Below is a partial listing of the headings and subdivisions found in the catalogue under "Ohio." Included are some of the subdivisions of most value to local and family history researchers. Note that not every entry refers to the state of Ohio:

> Ohio--Bibliography
> Ohio--Church History
> Ohio Company
> Ohio County, Indiana
> Ohio County, West Virginia
> Ohio--Description and Travel--Gazetteers
> The Ohio Frontier of 1812 (book title)
> Ohio--Genealogy
> Ohio--History
> Ohio--History, Local
> Ohio--History--Periodicals
> Ohio--History--1787-1865
> Ohio--History--Civil War
> Ohio in Short Stories, 1824-1839 (book title)
> Ohio--Registers of Births, etc. (refers
>   to births, deaths and marriages)
> Ohio River
> Ohio Valley

Each book in The Newberry Library should have a title card, an author card, and one or more subject cards. The most reliable way to locate a book is to check under the author's name, since a number of Newberry books catalogued in the past lack title cards. That leaves searching the catalogues by subject, which is what most researchers must do, as they seldom are seeking specific titles. Be imaginative when doing subject searches and assume that what you want will be in the Library.

The *Library of Congress Subject Headings,* 9th ed. (1980) can be helpful in determining what words can and cannot be used as subject headings. For example, "Coats of Arms" is not a correct subject heading; "Heraldry" or "Devices" is. Works on unions will be found under the subject heading "Trade-Unions," not "Labor Unions." Many topics are difficult to identify, or may be found under several possible subject headings. For example, one seeking a book that would identify place names in New York, might find relevant works under two different subject headings: "Names, Geographical--New York" and "New York--Description and Travel--Gazetteers." An excellent example of the need to be creative is in the case of works on land and land records, a subject of great importance to local and family history researchers. Relevant material can be found under the subject headings "Land Grants," "Land Titles," "Land Tenure," and geographical locations. Several different subdivisions within the geographical subject heading may yield works on land and land records. These include Public Lands, Deeds, Land Grants, Real Property, Genealogy, and Land Tenure. Another useful subject heading often overlooked by local and family history researchers is "Frontier and Pioneer Life."

Researchers must also be careful when seeking information on a particular geographical area. For example, if one were interested in Hammond, Indiana and looked in the catalogues only under "Hammond, Indiana," relevant material under "Indiana," "Lake County, Indiana," and "Calumet Region, Indiana" would be missed. The regional and area designations are especially tricky, but researchers must not forget about them. Below is a sample of just a few of the regional, area, mountain range, and valley designations that can be found:

Calumet Region, Indiana
Genesee Region, New York
Grand Traverse Region, Michigan
Northern Neck, Virginia
San Juan Mountains (Colorado and New Mexico)
San Joaquin Valley--California

Those seeking information on towns, counties, and local areas must also check under the name of the state. In many cases, relevant works on a county or town will appear only under the subject heading for the state. Returning to the example of Hammond, Indiana for a moment, the reader should refer to illustration A, a catalogue card for Timothy Ball's *Northwestern Indiana from 1800 to 1900.* This volume clearly contains information on Lake County, and presumably Hammond, but the book will be found in the Card Catalogue only under the subject heading "Indiana--History." A few other examples of this very common occurrence are Merrill D. Beal's *A History of Southeastern Idaho* (1942) and *Biographical and Historical Memoirs of Northeast Arkansas...* (1889), published by Goodspeed Publishing, both of which will be found only under the respective subject headings "Idaho--History" and "Arkansas--History."

One other card catalogue may also be of use to researchers. This is the Shelflist, which is arranged in call number order. Since Newberry patrons cannot browse through the bookstacks, the Shelflist compensates for this by allowing patrons to browse through the catalogue cards, arranged in the same order in which the books appear on the shelf. If a patron finds a book of interest and wishes to know what other books are shelved around it, the Shelflist provides a quick answer.

Finally, if all else fails, and you are unable to locate material which you think it is reasonable to expect the Newberry to have, please ask one of the reference librarians for assistance.

CHAPTER 2

PUBLISHED SOURCES AT THE NEWBERRY LIBRARY

NEWSPAPERS

Newspapers are important sources for local historians and genealogists. Researchers use accounts of newsworthy events, editorials, obituaries, and even advertisements to obtain information about individuals or some aspect of local history. The Newberry's newspaper holdings will be of most help to local historians and genealogists with research interests in the large cities in the East and Midwest. The library has lengthy runs of many eighteenth and nineteenth century newspapers, but there are few small-town papers in the collection. Newspaper research does present some problems. Genealogists, for example, who use newspapers to locate obituary notices, will find that these are uncommon before the 1880s. Another problem is that few newspapers are indexed, which often makes newspaper searches very time consuming.

Although the Newberry may not have the particular newspaper the researcher needs, it does have an extensive collection of reference books which will identify and guide the researcher to the needed newspaper. Winifred Gregory's *American Newspapers, 1821-1936* (1937, reprinted 1967), although fifty years old and out of date, is still the best overall guide to American newspapers. For newspapers before 1821, researchers should consult *History and Bibliography of American Newspapers, 1704-1820* (1947, plus 1961 supplement) by Clarence S. Brigham. In addition to these general works, there are many specialized bibliographies such as *Indiana Newspaper Bibliography...1804-1980* (1982) by John W. Miller; Stephen Gutgesell's *Guide to Ohio Newspapers, 1793-1973* (2nd ed., 1976); and *Swedish-American Newspapers: A Guide to the Microfilms Held by Swenson Swedish Immigration Research Center, Augustana College, Rock Island, Illinois* (1981), compiled by Lilly Setterdahl. Although most newspapers lack published indexes, many unpublished indexes exist in libraries and historical societies. Anita Cheek Milner has produced three volumes on newspaper indexes and their whereabouts: *Newspaper Indexes: A Location and Subject Guide for Researchers* (1977-82).

One of the most popular areas of genealogical publishing at the present time is the indexing and abstracting of genealogical information from newspapers. The Newberry actively collects works of this type, even though few of the newspapers are in the Newberry collection. Some examples are *Genealogical Data from the Pennsylvania Chronicle, 1767-1774* (1971) by Kenneth Scott; *Index to Marriage Notices in the Religious Herald, Richmond, Virginia, 1828-1938* (1941); and *Index to the Subjects of Obituaries Abstracted from Der Christliche Botschafter of the Evangelical Church, 1836-1866* (1967), by Dorothea Z. Seder.

The Newberry Library's single largest collection of newspapers is found in the *Microprint Edition of Early American Newspapers, 1704-1820*. This collection reproduces on microcards all extant issues of every newspaper published during this period. Over two hundred newspapers are included. They are all listed in the Card Catalogue under the heading "Early American Newspapers," as well as individually under their titles. This series is now beginning to include newspapers published after 1820 and now appears on microfilm. Many of the newspapers reproduced in this set are also available at the Library on microfilm, as facsimile copies, and, in some cases, in original newsprint editions.

In general, the library has few newspapers in the post-1900 period (Chicago being one exception). There are substantial runs of several Boston and New York papers for the late eighteenth and early nineteenth centuries. In addition to Boston and New York, runs of twenty-five years or more are available for Baltimore; Springfield, Massachusetts; Salem, Massachusetts; Detroit; Cincinnati; Burlington, Vermont; and Charleston, South Carolina.

One area in which the Newberry does have a good newspaper collection is in so-called "Frontier Newspapers." Published during the pioneer period, many of these papers were short-lived, but are important sources of information. A few representative titles include the *Arkansas Gazette, Florida Argus, St. Louis Reveille, Oquawka Spectator* (Illinois), *Council Bluffs Bugle, Charles Cist's Weekly Advertiser* (Cincinnati), *Deseret News* (Salt Lake City), *The Mountaineer* (Salt Lake City), and *Pioneer and Democrat* (Olympia, Washington). In addition, the library has a few scattered nineteenth century newspapers from Western Canada.

Chicago newspapers are heavily used by Newberry researchers, although, with the exception of German language newspapers, the library's holdings are by no means complete, or even the best in the city. The library does have at least one major newspaper for each year up to 1964 when all newspaper subscriptions ceased. Many of the newspapers are on microfilm, and some original papers are in fragile condition, making their use restricted. Restrictions are also imposed on the use of original pre-Chicago Fire (pre-1871) newspapers. The Newberry has the following major Chicago newspapers:

> *Chicago Tribune,* 1849-84, 1928-64.
> *Chicago Daily News,* 1877-1935.
> *Chicago Record,* 1881-1901.
> *Interocean,* 1874-1914.
> *Chicago Herald,* 1893-1919,
> *Chicago Times,* 1857-94.
> *Chicago Journal,* 1854-90.
> *Chicago Republican,* 1865-72 (one of the
> few complete runs of this newspaper in
> the country and an important source
> of financial news).
> *Chicago Weekly Journal,* 1847-94.

Please note that some issues of these newspapers are missing. An incomplete index to marriages and death notices from Chicago newspapers can be found in a manuscript (on microfilm) by Sam Fink, "Marriages and Deaths, Chicago Newspapers 1834-1889." Ten newspapers were searched for this index. The Chicago Genealogical Society has also published *Vital Records from Chicago Newspapers* (1971+), which presently numbers seven volumes covering 1833-48.

The Newberry Library does have the best newspaper collection for nineteenth century German language newspapers published in Chicago. The *Illinois Staats-Zeitung* is probably the best known German language newspaper. The Newberry's holdings cover 1861-1901 and are especially important because they include pre-Chicago Fire issues. Two other important newspapers are *Die Freie Presse* (1872-1898), for which the library has both weekly and Sunday editions, as well as the daily edition, and *Chicagoer Arbeiter Zeitung* (1879-89), which provides much information on the labor movement.

JOURNALS AND PERIODICALS

A wealth of information lies in local history and genealogy journals, and researchers will find the Newberry journal collection particularly strong. Journals are often overlooked sources because the information they contain is sometimes difficult to locate and identify; however, tools do exist to help researchers, and all standard guides, directories, indexes, and lists of historical and genealogical periodicals will be found at the Newberry.

Among the most important indexes and abstracts are *Writings in American History* (1902+) (the early volumes in particular); *America: History and Life* (1964+), which provides abstracts of articles and is a good source of local history journals, although few genealogical journals are included; *Index to Genealogical Periodicals* by Donald Lines Jacobus, which covers up to 1952; *Genealogical Periodical Annual Index* (1962+); and Kip Sperry's *Index to Genealogical Periodical Literature, 1960-1977* (1979). For further information on gaining access to genealogical periodical literature, see Kip Sperry's *A Survey of American Genealogical Periodicals and Periodical Indexes* (1978).

To locate journals and periodicals at The Newberry Library one can check the Card Catalogue for the title of the journal, or one can check by subject: "[Name of Place]--History (or Genealogy)--Periodicals." For example, under "San Luis Obispo Co., Calif.--History--Periodicals" one will find *La Vista,* the journal of the San Luis Obispo County Historical Society. The Newberry also maintains a "Check List of Journals Currently Received in The Newberry Library," which is available at several locations in the library.

Most journals are available in complete runs, a very important feature that facilitates research. In addition, the library's holdings are also quite strong for nineteenth and twentieth century journals which have ceased publication, including many which were short-lived. The library collects journals from all parts of the United States and Canada and maintains collections of all state and provincial historical society periodicals, plus many local (county and city) historical journals. The library's journal collection includes all major genealogical journals from all parts of the country. The library does not attempt to collect all local and county genealogical society journals, except those published by Illinois genealogical societies. Still many local genealogical society journals can be found among the holdings, but genealogical society newsletters are not collected. No attempt will be made to list every local historical and genealogical journal held by the Newberry, although many are mentioned in other sections of this guide.

Many foreign journals are available at the Newberry. The holdings of genealogical and local historical journals for Great Britain and Ireland are particularly strong. These include journals of national importance such as *Local Historian* (vol. 6+, 1963+) and *Genealogists'*

Magazine (1925+), as well as publications of local historical, genealogical, and antiquarian societies. The Newberry has a few German genealogical and heraldic journals, but no local history journals. Some French local and regional history journals are available, including ones for Avignon, Bordeaux, Bretagne, Burgundy, Normandy, and Provance. A few pre-World War II Italian local history journals are also part of the collection.

In addition to local history and genealogy journals, family newsletters and magazines may also prove useful to researchers. Most of these are privately published and in general are short-lived and/or erratic in publication, although some (*The Sparks Quarterly*, for example, which has appeared regularly since 1953) have long publishing histories. Because of their erratic nature, the library subscribes to few family periodicals, although many are received as gifts. Some of the well-established ones are catalogued and can be located under the family name in the Card Catalogue. Most are part of the Local and Family History Vertical File. For information on the Vertical File see Chapter 9.

Ethnic studies journals are another journal category useful to local and family history researchers. Some examples from the Newberry are the *Swedish-American Historical Quarterly* (formerly the *Swedish Pioneer Historical Quarterly*, 1950+), *Journal of the Afro-American Historical and Genealogical Society* (1980+), *Polish-American Studies* (1944+), and *Italian Americana* (1974+).

Researchers will find one other type of periodical useful--popular, nineteenth-century magazines and reviews from the United States and Great Britain. These journals provide background information and the "feel of the times" which can add a great deal to historical writing. The Newberry's holdings of these magazines are excellent. *North American Review, Blackwood's Edinburgh Magazine, Godey's Lady's Book, Eclectic Magazine* (New York), *Lakeside Monthly* (Chicago), and *Cornhill Magazine* (London) are just a few of the numerous nineteenth century magazines researchers can find at The Newberry Library.

DIRECTORIES

Directories, which list inhabitants of cities, small towns, counties, and rural areas, have long been used by historians and family history researchers to establish an individual's residence, address, or occupation. Directories can be used to discover what people were doing between censuses, and information from directories can often help save time when doing census searches. In addition to information about individuals, directories contain demographic data; even the advertisements and lists of churches, schools, and organizations can be rich sources of information about a community and the times.

City directories first appeared in the United States in the late 1700s. Philadelphia was the first city to have a separately published directory--

two different ones were published for the city in 1785. The Newberry has original editions of the first directories of several cities including Chicago (1839), Cincinnati (1819), Cleveland (1837), Detroit (1837), Kansas City (1859), Milwaukee (1847), Omaha (1866), Peoria, Illinois (1844), and St. Louis (1821), and facsimiles of the first directory for several other cities.

Most directories in The Newberry Library are not catalogued. They are listed in a separate City Directory Card File, which is arranged alphabetically by city, town, or county. But some directories do appear in the Card Catalogue. These include all directories published before 1860, as well as some published after that time. In other words, researchers must be sure to check both the Card Catalogue and the City Directory Card File. In addition, all pre-1800 directories are available on microcards in the Readex Microprint Edition of Evans' Early American Imprints. The Newberry also has on microfiche all pre-1860 directories for Illinois, Indiana, Iowa, Ohio, and Kentucky. For a listing of all pre-1860 directories see Dorothea N. Spear's *American Directories Through 1860* (1961).

The directory holdings at the Newberry cover all parts of the United States, large cities, small towns, counties, and rural areas. Most of the directories date from 1870 to 1930, although a great many will be found for years prior to 1870. The Newberry does not collect directories after 1930. A small collection of social registers is available for about two dozen cities throughout the country. The collection for Chicago, which begins in 1894, is the largest. Nearly all the social registers are from the twentieth century, with many from the post-1930 period. There are a few directories for foreign cities. A number of Post Office Directories are available for London between 1873 and 1930, as well as the Amsterdam directory for 1885/86, and some Berlin directories between the years 1893 and 1914. The library has few Canadian directories except some from Montreal.

The Newberry has all the Chicago directories, which date from 1839 to 1928/29 available on microfilm. Directories were not published in some years, while in other years two competing directories were published. No alphabetical directories were published after 1928/29. There are three directories for Chicago arranged by ADDRESS ONLY for the years 1952, 1953, and 1955. Chicago telephone books are part of the Newberry collection, although they are very fragile and must be handled with extreme care. The Newberry's holdings cover 1914-60 and 1970-80. The library also has some classified and suburban telephone directories.

Below is a partial sampling of cities for which The Newberry Library has sizeable runs of directories. The inclusive dates *do not* indicate that the library has a directory for every year, rather they indicate that a reasonably good run is available.

Albany, New York, 1840-1930
Baltimore 1865, 1875, 1893-1927
Boston 1789 (facsimile), 1805, 1836-1929
Buffalo, New York, 1828, 1837, 1847,
    1848, 1853, 1863-1928
Cambridge, Massachusetts, 1848, 1857,
    1863/64, 1885-1900, 1918
Cincinnati All pre-1860 directories on
    microfiche, 1819, 1829, 1836/37,
    1842, 1843, 1860-78, 1892-1927/28
Cleveland All pre-1860 directories on
    microfiche, 1837, 1846/47, 1856,
    1893-1927
Denver 1859 (facsimile), 1885-1928
Des Moines, Iowa, 1907-28
Detroit 1837, 1850, 1866-75, 1892-1928
District of Columbia 1876, 1878,
    1892-1927
Evanston, Illinois, 1884, 1892-1929, 1935, 1937
Fargo, North Dakota, 1881-1927(on microfiche)
Fort Wayne, Indiana, All pre-1860 directories on
    microfiche, 1861/62, 1868/69, 1896-1928
Haverhill, Massachusetts, 1857-1930
Indianapolis All pre-1860 directories on
    microfiche, 1855, 1857, 1881, 1892-1929
Joliet, Illinois, 1893, 1903-21, 1930
Kansas City 1859, 1860/61, 1892-1929
Los Angeles 1872 (facsimile), 1903-30
Louisville, Kentucky, All pre-1860 directories on
    microfiche, 1832, 1843/44, 1874, 1892-1930
Memphis, Tennessee, 1903-30
Milwaukee 1847/48-1851/52, 1863, 1877/78,
    1892-1927
Minneapolis 1887-1927
Montreal, Canada, 1881/82, 1892-1922/23
Moorhead, Minnesota, 1881-1927(microfiche)
New Haven, Connecticut, 1842-82, 1916-22/23
New Orleans 1871, 1875, 1892-1928
New York City 1786 (facsimile), 1798, 1808, 1811,
    1813, 1826, 1829-1933
Newark, New Jersey, 1835/36, 1840, 1847-75, 1894,
    1904-24
Omaha, Nebraska, 1866, 1892-1928
Peoria, Illinois, All pre-1860 directories on
    microfiche, 1844, 1856, 1861, 1876, 1903-30
Philadelphia 1811, 1813, 1839/40-1851/52, 1865-1927

Pittsburgh 1826, 1863-1878/79, 1892-1927
Providence, Rhode Island, 1824 (facsimile), 1844,
    1856, 1892-1927 Richmond, Virginia, 1819, 1866,
    1877-95, 1915-26
Rochester, New York, 1827, 1870-1928
Rockford, Illinois, All pre-1860 directories on
    microfiche, 1857, 1869, 1874/75, 1903-23
St. Louis 1821, 1869-1930
St. Paul, Minnesota, 1863-1869/70, 1885-1930
San Francisco 1850, 1856-60, 1874, 1893-1930
Seattle 1882, 1897-1930
Syracuse, New York, 1864/65, 1867/68, 1903-28
Toledo, Ohio, All pre-1860 directories on microfiche,
    1903-28
Waukegan, Illinois, 1892/93, 1903-29
Worcester, Massachusetts, 1844-1903, 1919

GENEALOGIES

The old saying, "You can't judge a book by its cover," could have been written with genealogies in mind. Despite the uneven quality of such works, which run from outstanding to awful, these volumes can be quite useful. Although most heavily consulted by genealogists, printed family histories can also solve problems for biographers, and can assist researchers studying social, political, and local history.

The earliest genealogy in book form was *Genealogy of the Family of Mr. Samuel Stebbins, and Mrs. Hannah Stebbins, His Wife, from the Year 1707, to the Year 1771*, printed in 1771. The Newberry has a facsimile of this book printed in 1879. An even earlier example of a family record printed in America is found in the *Memoirs of Capt. Roger Clap...* (1731), a copy of which is held by the Newberry. Interest in printing and publishing family histories grew slowly in the first half of the nineteenth century. By the end of the Civil War, about 300 genealogies had been printed. From that point on interest grew at a rapid pace until today it is estimated that 25,000 to 30,000 genealogies have been printed.

Genealogies At The Newberry Library

The Newberry's collection of genealogies numbers approximately 17,000 volumes, making it one of the larger collections in the United States. It is particularly strong for nineteenth and early twentieth century works. Of the first fourteen American genealogies published through 1837, the Newberry lacks only two.[1] In recent years the library has not attempted to collect every new genealogy, although it does add several hundred volumes each year. Many new works have been donated to the library, and although the Newberry is able to purchase

few genealogies, significant works, such as the Mayflower Society's Five Generation Project and books which have won awards, will be found in the collection.

Most genealogies at the Newberry deal with American families, but the library does have a number of British genealogies, primarily from the late nineteenth and early twentieth centuries. With the exception of Great Britain and Ireland, the library's holdings of foreign genealogies are quite small.

Although not every genealogy will be found at The Newberry Library, bibliographic tools exist that can identify titles of interest and locations where the books can be found. Marion J. Kaminkow has compiled two of the most important works: *Genealogies in the Library of Congress* (1972, plus 1977 supplement) and *A Complement to Genealogies in the Library of Congress* (1981), which lists genealogies found in forty-five library collections, not including the Newberry. Another valuable work is the New York Public Library's *Dictionary Catalog of the Local History and Genealogy Division,* 20 volumes (1974), which includes not only books, but also citations for many periodical articles. For bibliographies of British, Irish and Scottish genealogies see Chapters 17.

Unique Genealogies In The Newberry Collection

Over the years The Newberry Library has acquired typescripts, manuscripts, and working papers from many family historians. Much of this material is not catalogued and is part of the Local and Family History Section's Vertical File Collection. See Chapter 9 for further information on the Vertical File Collection. Although most of these collections are quite small, a few contain substantial amounts of material. Most of this material is unique to the Newberry, and in the hope of making its existence more widely known, the large collections are listed below. Please keep in mind that the quality varies, as does the usability. Few of these collections are indexed, and many are organized in only the most rudimentary fashion. Library staff members do attempt to answer queries regarding Vertical File material; however, for many of these large collections, a personal examination will be necessary.

Some of the unique genealogy collections at The Newberry Library are:

The Crispe Family by Thomas Edward Crispe, three boxes.

Typescripts of Arthur Leslie Keith on the Broyles, Cawood, Chenoweth, Clore/Glore, Keith, Wilhoit and Yager families.

The Knapp Family by Alfred Averill Knapp, four boxes.

The Leavitt Family by Joseph P. Leavitt, six boxes.

The McArthur Family by Dr. Selim W. McArthur, four boxes.

The Thomas Minor Family by William R. McGowan, eight boxes.

The Reasoner Family by Col. Mathew A. Reasoner, three boxes.

The Reid and Manierre Families by Julie Manierre Mann, six boxes.

Descendants of Ambroise Sicard by Frederick Secord, 13 volumes. This collection has been catalogued and is not part of the Vertical File.

The Witwer Family by Edward B. Witwer and Dorothy Witwer Stabler, seven boxes. Supplementary material to the *Witwer Geneaology* [sic] *of America* (1909), by Rev. George Witwer and Ananias Cline Witwer.

NOTES
1. Clarence S. Brigham, *Fifty Years of Collecting Americana for the Library of The American Antiquarian Society* (Worcester, Mass.: American Antiquarian Society, 1958), pp.67-8.

BIBLIOGRAPHIES AND INDEXES

One of the acknowledged strengths of The Newberry Library is its holdings of bibliographies. The collections in local and family history are no exception. While the researcher will not find every needed book at the Newberry, the outstanding collection of bibliographies will help researchers identify works of interest and aid them in locating copies at other institutions. Listed below are works of a general nature. Other bibliographies relating to local and family history (bibliographies of ethnic or religious groups, state and local history bibliographies) are mentioned elsewhere in this guide.

The largest printed list of books held by United States libraries is *The National Union Catalog (NUC)*. *NUC* is arranged by author or main entry and lists at least one library which holds the book in question. This is an essential tool for those seeking the location of a particular title, a list of books by a particular author, or the verification of citations.

In the area of family history, the most important work is P. William Filby's *American & British Genealogy & Heraldry: A Selected List of Books,* 3rd edition (1983). This volume contains listings for each state as well as special topics. It is a selective bibliography and the annotations are useful in evaluating sources. Another important contribution by Filby is *A Bibliography of American County Histories* (1985), which contains over 5,000 entries. Filby does exclude some "mug books" and certain municipal histories that may relate to the history of particular counties. One other general bibliography is *Genealogy and Local History Books in Print,* 4th edition (1985), compiled by Netti Schreiner-Yantis. Both new titles and reprints are included, and the inclusion of ordering information makes this work quite useful.

No library in the United States holds every book ever printed or published on local or family history, and there is no bibliography of such works that is one hundred percent complete. However, there are several bibliographies of major library collections which, when consulted together, provide fairly thorough coverage of the field. The Library of

Congress collection of local and family histories is one of the largest in the country, and two bibliographies by Marion J. Kaminkow list these holdings: *Genealogies in the Library of Congress* (1972, plus 1977 supplement) and *United States Local Histories in the Library of Congress* (1975). A third work by Kaminkow, *A Complement to Genealogies in the Library of Congress* (1981), lists genealogies found in forty-five major library collections excluding the Library of Congress and The Newberry. Another of the larger local and family history collections in this country is found at the New York Public Library. The *Dictionary Catalog of the Local History and Genealogy Division,* 20 volumes (1974) is another essential bibliographic source, especially since it includes citations for some periodical articles as well as books. The National Society, Daughters of the American Revolution is also issuing a catalogue of its library in Washington, D.C. Volume I, *Family Histories and Genealogies* (1982) has appeared. Other planned volumes will cover state and local histories and general works. Last, but certainly not least, of the library catalogues is the Genealogical Library Catalog (GLC), a catalog and guide to the holdings of the Church of Jesus Christ of Latter-day Saints (hereafter referred to as LDS) Genealogical Library in Salt Lake City. The GLC includes both printed works and records microfilmed throughout the world. It is on microfiche and is periodically updated. For further information see Chapter 10, "Source Material from the Genealogical Department of the Church of Jesus Christ of Latter-day Saints."

The Newberry has an excellent collection of biographical indexes and dictionaries, both old and new. One of the largest such works is *Biography and Genealogy Master Index,* 2nd edition (1980, plus 1981-85 cumulation), a multi-volume index to 350 current and retrospective biographical dictionaries. Researchers need to be aware that the library collects biographical dictionaries only in fields that correspond to its collecting areas. Thus, while researchers will find such works as *The Encyclopedia of Southern History* (1979), *Who's Who of the Colored Race* (1915, reprinted 1976), or *American Women: Fifteen Hundred Biographies with Over 1,400 Portraits* (1897, reprinted 1973), they will not find such works as current *Who's Who in Finance and Industry* or *The New York Times Encyclopedia of Television.*

The *American Genealogical-Biographical Index (AGBI),* begun in 1952, is a first and last name index to approximately 830 works in genealogy, local history, and military history. The Newberry lacks fewer than one hundred titles indexed in this series, only about a dozen of which are longer than one hundred pages. The first series of *AGBI* was published between 1942 and 1952, and the second, greatly expanded series, is still in progress. Two other indexes, although not as extensive as *AGBI,* should also be mentioned. The first is *The Library of Congress Index to Biographies in State and Local Histories.* This index, on forty reels of microfilm, contains approximately 170,000 cards taken from 340 titles. It is not clear what the criteria were for determining which books to include, and the coverage of the various states is quite uneven. The Newberry has the majority of the 340 titles, although its coverage is also uneven--very thorough for some states, poor for others. The second index is George R. Crowther's *Surname Index to 65 Volumes of Colonial and Revolutionary Pedigrees* (1964). The Newberry has only a few of the sixty-five volumes indexed in this work, since the Library lacks the twenty-seven volumes of *Colonial Families of America* and the twenty volumes of *Colonial and Revolutionary Lineages of America.*

One of the most important indexes for local and family historians is, of course, the *Genealogical Index of The Newberry Library.* This index is discussed in detail in Chapter 9, along with another Newberry indexing project, the "Chicago and Cook County Biography and Industry File."

One of the largest and most important sources of biographical and genealogical information held by the Newberry is the 1984 edition of the International Genealogical Index (IGI), an index to names found in computerized files of the Genealogical Department of the LDS Church. This microfiche set includes over 88 million names from over ninety countries. Entries are taken from government records (including records of births and marriages), selected records submitted by LDS members, parish registers, some LDS temple records, and other miscellaneous sources.

One other category of material which falls under the general heading of "indexes" is genealogical query columns in newspapers. Two of these are of particular importance. The *Boston Evening Transcript Genealogy Column* appeared between 1896 and 1941, and is being indexed in *AGBI.* It is available at the Newberry on microcards. The *Hartford Times Genealogy Column* for February, 1934 to May, 1967 is on microfilm, and the queries have been rearranged in alphabetical order. Several smaller genealogy columns, such as "Michiana Roots," which appears in the South Bend, Indiana, *Tribune,* beginning in 1973, can also be found at the Newberry.

U.S. GOVERNMENT PUBLICATIONS

United States government publications are a rich resource for local and family historians, but many researchers fail to use them because they do not recognize their importance or know how to identify and locate them. All government publications at The Newberry Library, with the exception of the *U. S. Serial Set,* can be located in the Card Catalogue both under the name of the agency from which the document originated and under the appropriate subject headings. The name of the originating agency takes the place of an author entry. Some typical agency entries are "U.S.--Bureau of the Census," "U. S.--Library of Congress," and "U.S.--War Department." Researchers should know that government publications have a unique classification system, which means they will have call numbers quite different from those found on other library books. Several problems may arise when using old government publications: originating agencies may have been transferred from one department to another, titles of series may change, agencies may cease to exist, and new agencies are created. Mastery of United States government publications requires much study and effort, and this chapter can highlight only some of the most important sources for local and family historians and suggest some uses for government publications.[2]

Many libraries in the United States are designated as U.S. Government Depositories and receive regular shipments of government publications. The Newberry was a Government Depository Library until 1921, and, although the library continues to acquire many government publications, researchers will find that some serial publications are only available through 1921.

A very important government publication is the *American State Papers* (1832-61). The *American State Papers* contains the most important legislative and executive documents from the first fourteen congresses from 1789 to 1838. It consists of thirty-eight volumes divided into ten classes. The most useful classes for local and family historians are Class 8, Public Lands and Class 9, Claims. These cover land claims, pre-emption titles, bounty lands, petitions for extra pay, and compensation for services and goods.

Two publications index information in the *American State Papers,* and I recommend that both works be consulted, as some discrepancies exist between the two. *Grassroots of America* (1972), edited by Phillip W. McMullin, is a name index to the Public Lands and Claims classes. *CIS U. S. Serial Set Index* (1975-79) indexes both the *Serial Set* and the *American State Papers*. One other point of confusion makes using the *American State Papers* difficult. Class 8, Public Lands, was issued by two different printers. Gales and Seaton issued an eight-volume set, which is considered to be the standard one, and Duff Green issued a five-volume set. The two sets are not identical, and *CIS U. S. Serial Set Index* and *Grassroots of America* index the Gales and Seaton printing. The Newberry has all but volume 31 of the Gales and Seaton printing, and volumes 2, 3, and 4 (29, 30, and 31) of the Duff Green printing. Volume 4 of the Duff Green printing is volume 31 in the Newberry's set of *American State Papers,* and citations to volume 31 from the two indexes may be difficult or impossible to find.

A second important government publication is the *U. S. Serial Set,* which does not appear in the Card Catalogue (except for some individual volumes, most of which are part of the Graff and Ayer collections). The set begins with the 15th Congress (1817-18), and the Newberry's holdings end with the 66th Congress (1920-21). The Newberry set contains volumes 1 to 7913 (a few volumes are missing). The *Serial Set* is a selective compilation of congressional publications, executive branch publications, and certain non-government publications. Included are many items relevant to local and family history such as claims and petitions, private bills, reports of military expeditions to the West, maps, and selected annual reports of non-government agencies including the D. A. R. and various veterans organizations.

The easiest access to the *Serial Set* is through *CIS U. S. Serial Set Index.* The Newberry has the first twenty-four volumes which cover through the 68th Congress (1925). This is not an every-name index, except for those cited as "recipients of proposed relief or related actions by Congress." The library also has other earlier indexes to government publications including Ben Perley Poore's *A Descriptive Catalogue of the Government Publications of the United States, September 5, 1774-March 4, 1881* (1885, reprinted 1953) and *Comprehensive Index to the Publications of the United States Government, 1881-1893* (1905, reprinted 1953) by John G. Ames, both of which include publications in addition to the *Serial Set.*

The third important government publication is *The Territorial Papers of the United States,* 28 volumes (1934+). *The Territorial Papers* cover, geographically, all the states of the Northwest Territory, Mississippi, Louisiana, Missouri, Alabama, Arkansas and Florida. The volumes contain correspondence and reports of government officials, maps and many petitions by inhabitants. For example, in volume 28 for Wisconsin, there is an 1846 petition of the settlers on Rock River and the Milwaukee Canal Tract signed by over 500 settlers (pp. 999-1013) and an 1840 petition for a new post road from Fort Winnebago to Plover Portage Mills, signed by over 100 inhabitants of the Pineries of the Upper Wisconsin River (pp. 105-7).

Information on many individuals, including those who submitted private claims to Congress between 1774 and 1789, can be found in the journals and papers of the Continental Congress. The Newberry does have *Journals of the Continental Congress, 1774-1789,* 34 volumes (1904-37), but does not have the microfilm publication of *Papers of the Continental Congress.* The library does, however, have the published indexes to both the Journals and the Papers: *The Index: Journals of the Continental Congress, 1774-1789* (1976) compiled by Kenneth E. Harris and Steven D. Tilley and *Index: The Papers of the Continental Congress, 1774-1789,* 5 volumes (1978), compiled by John P. Butler. One other source of private claims is *Digested Summary and Alphabetical List of Private Claims...to the House of Representatives from the First to the Thirty-first Congress* (1970), which is a reprint of volumes 653-55 of the *Serial Set.* All names in this volume should appear in the *CIS Index.*

Annual Report of the Smithsonian Institution, Annual Report of the American Historical Association, congressional directories, U. S. census statistical reports, service academy registers, *Official Army Register* (1813+, some volumes missing), and *Navy Register* (1825+, some volumes missing) are just a few of the additional government publications that await researchers at The Newberry Library.

NOTES

2. An excellent guide to government publications, which contains much historical information, is Laurence F. Schmeckebier and Roy B. Eastin, *Government Publications and Their Use,* 2nd rev. ed. (Washington: Brookings Institution, 1969).

SURNAMES

Local and family history researchers often want to know the origin and meaning of various surnames. They may also need information on name changes, including legal changes of name, evolutionary change, and the transformation of foreign surnames to English equivalents. The Newberry Library holds works on all these aspects of names. In keeping with the geographical limits of the Newberry's overall collection policy, surname books concentrate on North America, Western Europe, and Latin America. The library has a small collection of books on given or Christian names.

Books on surnames are found in the Card Catalogue under "Names, Personal--[Name of country, geographical area or nationality]." Some works found under this subject heading deal with philology and will be of limited use to local historians and genealogists. The Newberry in 1901 purchased the Bonaparte Collection on linguistics amassed by Prince Louis-Lucien Bonaparte. The Bonaparte Collection is housed in the Department of Special Collections.

Most books dealing with the origin and meaning of surnames are limited to a single country or nationality. The best attempt at a comprehensive list of surnames and their meanings is Elsdon C. Smith's, *New Dictionary of American Family Names* (1973), which contains over 10,000 brief entries. A useful bibliography for the surname researcher is Smith's *Personal Names, A Bibliography* (1952), which includes only English language works.

The English have been especially interested in surnames, and the Newberry collection for Great Britain is very strong. The English Surnames Series (1973+) for local areas of England is available, as well as standard works such as Percy H. Reaney's *A Dictionary of British Surnames* (2nd ed., 1976), Cecil H. L'Estrange Ewen's *History of Surnames of the British Isles* (1931), and the works of Charles W. E. Bardsley. Edward MacLysaght's *The Surnames of Ireland* (1969) and George F. Black's *The Surnames of Scotland* (1946), are but two of the many works found on those countries.

Important books on the surnames of Western Europe include works by Albert Dauzat on French surnames. *Toponimos en Apellidos Hispanos* (1968) by Grace de Jesus C. Alvarez is very good for Spanish surnames. The library has many books on Spanish and Latin American surnames. The Newberry holds several titles on Germanic surnames including *Deutsche Namenkunde,* 5 volumes (1952-56), by Adolf Bach; *Die*

Deutschen Familiennamen, Geschichtlich, Geographisch, Sprachlich (1925), by Albert Heintze and Paul Cascorbi; and the works of Josef Brechenmacher. One of the most comprehensive works on Italian surnames is *Our Italian Surnames* (1949) by Joseph C. Fucilla. Although Fucilla's book is in English, researchers should be aware that most surname books on non-English-speaking countries are not in English.

Books dealing with name changes are found under the same subject heading in the Card Catalogue as books on the origin and meaning of surnames. Some examples of these works are *Divorces and Names Changed in Maryland by Act of the Legislature 1634-1854* (1970) by Mary Keysor Meyer and *Some Anglicized Surnames in Ireland* (1923) by Patrick Downey.

PUBLICATIONS OF THE WORKS PROGRESS ADMINISTRATION

Between 1935 and 1943 the Works Progress Administration (called Work Projects Administration after 1939) provided employment to millions of out-of-work Americans. People worked in construction, school lunch rooms, on conservation projects, in household training programs, and, happily for local historians and genealogists, on local historical and archival projects. Three WPA projects--the Historical Records Survey, the Federal Writers' Project, and the Historic American Buildings Survey--are of particular importance. The Newberry has only a few publications from the Historic American Buildings Survey; consequently, this chapter will be devoted to publications of the Historical Records Survey (HRS) and the Federal Writers' Project (FWP).

During the Great Depression the Historical Records Survey indexed, inventoried, and transcribed numerous records. Although some of this work remains unpublished, between 1936 and 1943, the HRS produced several hundred mimeographed guides, directories, and inventories. Despite the passage of over forty years, many of these publications are not outdated and have not been superseded.

The *Check List of Historical Records Survey Publications* (1943, reprinted 1969), by Sargent B. Child and Dorothy P. Holmes, lists HRS Publications. They are found in the Card Catalogue under "Historical Records Survey--[Name of State]," as well as under their respective subject headings. Loretta L. Hefner's *The WPA Historical Records Survey: A Guide to the Unpublished Inventories, Indexes, and Transcripts* (1980) is helpful in identifying additional HRS compilations and projects.

The Newberry holdings of HRS publications are very good. There are works for all forty-eight states and the District of Columbia. Although some of the publications contain transcripts of record sources (many of the Newberry's compilations of vital records, marriages, and court records were first done by the HRS), most are directories, guides, or inventories of archival and manuscript collections which do not contain the information itself, but direct the researcher to that information. The following categories of HRS publications are of most interest to local and family historians: inventories of church archives, inventories of newspapers, transcriptions of public archives, inventories of county archives (these often contain useful bibliographies), American imprints inventories, directories of churches and religious organizations, guides to public vital statistics, calendars of manuscript collections, and guides to church vital statistics records. Some typical examples from the Newberry collection are: *Inventory of the Church Archives of Alabama...Protestant Episcopal Church* (1939), *The Cuyuna Range; a History of a Minnesota Iron Mining District* (1940), *Directory of Churches and Religious Organizations in Maine* (1940), *Minutes of the County Court of Knox County* [Tennessee]. *Book No. "O," 1792-95* (1941), and *Inventory of the County Archives of Nebraska...Gosper County* (1940).

One task of the Federal Writers' Project was the compilation of guides describing each state and its major cities, and outlining tours. Other FWP publications dealt with local history, slave narratives, folklore, social conditions, and ethnic material. Many of these are part of the American Guide Series. The library's holdings of FWP publications are not quite as good as the holdings of HRS publications, but many of the state guides and other historical works are available. These can be identified in the Card Catalogue under the headings "American Guide Series," "Federal Writers' Project," and "Writers' Program." They will, of course, also be found under the appropriate subject headings. Two bibliographies of FWP publications are Evanell K. Powell's *WPA Writers' Publications: A Complete Bibliographic Check List and Price Guide...of the Federal Writers' Project and Program* (1974), and *Catalogue: WPA Writers' Program Publications* (September 1941) by the Work Projects Administration. Some representative FWP titles from the Newberry collection are: *Shorewood* [Wisconsin] (1939), *New Hampshire, A Guide to the Granite State* (1938), *Erie;* [Pennsylvania] *A Guide to the City and County* (1938), and *The Armenians in Massachusetts* (1937).

MAPS, ATLASES, AND GEOGRAPHICAL SOURCES

Genealogists and local historians are often faced with questions that must be answered by a map, atlas, gazetteer, or place name guide. Such sources can be used to determine correct county, town, or city ward of residence so that the proper records (including census schedules) can be searched; for locating farms and lands owned; and for identifying locations that no longer exist or have changed names.

Researchers at The Newberry Library will find an outstanding collection of maps and geographical sources. The staff of the Newberry's Map Section is very knowledgeable and should be consulted to avoid wasting time searching the wrong geographical sources. If one has the name of a town and knows only that it is (or was) in Texas, poring over a detailed map of Texas is a very inefficient way to locate the place. In this case, it would be much better to consult a Texas gazetteer or place name guide, determine the location, then locate it on a map.

Researchers must look for maps in *two* places--the Card Catalogue and the Map Catalogue. To find maps and atlases in the Card Catalogue look under the heading "[Name of place]--Maps." The Map Catalogue is divided into three sections: geographical area, name of cartographer, and title of the map. Place name guides and gazetteers often cover much of the same ground, and researchers are wise to check under subject headings for both types of works. For gazetteers look under "[Name of place]--Description and Travel--Gazetteers." For place name guides look under "Names, Geographical--[Name of place]." Another related source not to be overlooked is books that list post offices. These can be found in the Card Catalogue under the heading "Postal Service--[Name of place]."

Another common error of map researchers is overlooking modern maps, atlases, and gazetteers. These works should be consulted first as they often provide the simplest answer to a map or geography question. For world atlases, the *The Times Atlas of the World* and the *Pergamon World Atlas* are good places to begin. A companion to these is the current *Columbia Lippincott Gazetteer of the World.* The Newberry also has the U.S. Board on Geographic Names, Gazetteer Series. This series, in sixty-seven parts, was published between 1955 and 1962 and provides "official standard names" for many countries throughout the world. An older world atlas, which is an excellent source for those trying to locate towns in Europe around the turn of the century, is Richard Andree's *Andrees Allgemeiner Handatlas* (1893). This atlas is especially useful because it uses the "old" names for towns and cities and has a rather extensive place name index. For researchers seeking to locate towns in the German Empire in the nineteenth and early twentieth centuries, three gazetteers that may provide help are: *Neumanns Orts- und Verkehrs-Lexikon des Deutschen Reichs* (1905), *Meyers Lexikon, Orts- und Verkehrslexikon des Deutschen Reiches,* 7th edition (1935), and the world gazetteer, *Ritters Geographisch- Statistisches Lexikon* (1905-06).

The Newberry's collection of geographical sources is quite varied, both in geographical coverage and type of material. The library has thousands of maps and atlases, in various scales, covering most of North America and Western Europe. These maps are of many different types--topographical, land ownership, transportation, commercial, and military. The library's collection of nineteenth century county land ownership atlases is good, and reprints of these are actively acquired.

At the present time, there is no definitive bibliography of county atlases, and Clara LeGear's *United States Atlases,* 2 volumes (1950-53), remains the best listing. Researchers should also not forget about bird's-eye views. The Newberry has few original bird's-eye views, but there are a number of facsimiles in the collection, including those published by the firm Historic Urban Plans. Bird's-eye views can be identified in the Map Catalogue under "[Name of place]--Views." A fine bibliography of city and town views has been compiled by John W. Reps, *Views and Viewmakers of Urban America: Lithographs of Towns and Cities in the United States and Canada, Notes on the Artists and Publishers, And a Union Catalog of Their Work, 1825-1925* (1984).

A very fine collection of nineteenth and twentieth century gazetteers and place name guides is available. A list of place name guides for the United States and Canada is found in *Bibliography of Place-Name Literature, United States and Canada,* 3rd edition (1982), by Richard B. Sealock, Margaret M. Sealock, and Margaret S. Powell.

Although the library does not have every map and atlas needed by researchers, it does have an excellent collection of map bibliographies which will help researchers determine if a map they need exists. Many map bibliographies of individual states have been published, and researchers working in the Midwest are especially fortunate to have the *Checklist of Printed Maps of the Middle West to 1900* (1981-83), edited by Robert W. Karrow, Jr., the Newberry's Curator of Maps. This fourteen-volume set covers Illinois, Indiana, Iowa, Kansas, Michigan, Minnesota, Missouri, Nebraska, North Dakota, Ohio, South Dakota, and Wisconsin.

Another work of importance, also prepared at The Newberry Library, is the *Historical Atlas and Chronology of County Boundaries, 1788-1980,* 5 volumes (1984), edited by John H. Long. This set is an outgrowth of the United States Historical County Boundary Data File Project at the Newberry and records every change in county boundaries for fourteen states. Excellent introductory essays on the boundary history of each area are included, as well as bibliographies of boundary changes. The fourteen states covered are Delaware, Maryland, New Jersey, Pennsylvania, Illinois, Indiana, Ohio, Michigan, Wisconsin, Iowa, Missouri, Minnesota, North Dakota, and South Dakota.

The Newberry now has available a very large and important set of nearly 1500 nineteenth century county land ownership maps from the Library of Congress. These maps, on microfiche, include both manuscript and printed maps, and at least a few are available for most states. The northeast, north-central states, Virginia, California, and Texas are especially well covered. For a listing of the maps, researchers should consult Richard W. Stephenson's *Land Ownership Maps: A Checklist of the 19th Century United States County Maps in the Library of Congress* (1967).

Ward Maps of United States Cities: A Selective Checklist of Pre-1900

Maps in the Library of Congress is an extremely valuable source for those doing census searches in cities. Compiled by Michael H. Shelley, this microfiche set has 232 maps of thirty-five cities.

One other set deserves mention as it is rarely used and can be quite useful, especially to those doing research in an area which was the site of military activity during the Civil War. This is the *Atlas to Accompany the Official Records of Union and Confederate Armies* (1891-95), a series of maps done by the U. S. Engineers during the Civil War. The maps are very detailed, and many show residences with names of occupants and other cultural features such as churches. The Newberry's Map Section is currently working on a graphic index to these maps.

The Newberry's map collection includes a number of nineteenth and early twentieth century medium- and large-scale maps of the countries of Western Europe. One of the most significant is the *Ordnance Townland Survey of Ireland*, complete in 33 volumes (1831-46). The very large scale of this set, six inches to the mile, provides an incredibly detailed view of Ireland in the mid-1800s. The library also has a set of Irish maps on a scale of one inch to the mile. The nineteenth century Ordnance Survey of England, Wales and Scotland is available in a reprint on a scale of one inch to the mile. (A modern version, at a scale of one quarter inch to a mile, is also part of the library's collection.) Good detailed maps for Germany are found in the official set of *Topographische Karten*, published between 1918 and 1927. Other countries for which the library has medium- to large-scale maps from the nineteenth and twentieth centuries include Belgium, Denmark, France, Iceland, Italy, the Netherlands, Norway, Spain, and Sweden.

CHAPTER 3

CENSUS MATERIALS

Census materials are among the most valuable research sources. Of first importance are the federal population schedules, but other sources such as federal non-population schedules, statistical reports, and state censuses should not be overlooked.

FEDERAL POPULATION CENSUS MICROFILMS

The microfilmed federal census population schedules at the Newberry have not been catalogued and will not be found by searching the Card Catalogue, but appear in guides found in the General Reading Room. The Newberry has many, but not all, available census microfilms. Coverage is most complete for the midwestern states. The collection is complete for the entire country for the years 1800, 1810, 1820, 1830, 1850, and 1890. The 1840 schedules are being acquired, and the 1870 schedules are complete for the southern and border states, and most of the Midwest. In addition, the states of Colorado, Illinois, Indiana, Iowa, Ohio, Oregon, and Wisconsin are complete through 1880. The library also holds the 1900 census for Illinois and Alaska, and the 1910 schedules for Illinois. Holdings of 1900 and 1910 schedules for other states are limited.

Indexes and Soundex
The library is in the final stages of completing its holdings of all

available state-wide census indexes through the 1850 census. These are part of the Local and Family History Open Shelf Collection. Few state-wide indexes have been published for the post-1850 censuses, and most of them will be found at the Newberry. In addition to the state-wide indexes, there are indexes for many individual counties. For example, nearly every Illinois county has been indexed individually for 1860. Many county indexes will be found on the Local and Family History Open Shelf, but all can be located in the Card Catalogue under the heading "[Name of County]--Census, [Year of Census]" (e.g., Piatt County, Illinois--Census, 1860).

The Newberry holds the following Soundex indexes to the federal census: 1880--Indiana, Illinois, and Iowa; 1900--Illinois. The library does not have the 1910 Soundex for Illinois.

Special Finding Aids for Chicago

Because of its large population, Chicago has presented many problems for researchers consulting census records. To help increase the success rate and reduce the amount of time spent searching census microfilms, the Local and Family History Section has developed finding aids that locate people by address for the 1870, 1880, 1900 and 1910 Chicago censuses. These aids are only helpful if an individual's address is known, either from a contemporary city directory or some other source. Even though Soundex indexes exist for the 1880 and later Illinois censuses, many people who in fact are enumerated in the schedules fail to appear on the Soundex or are listed under incorrect codes.

For the 1880, 1900, and 1910 censuses, maps have been prepared showing enumeration district boundaries. An address is pinpointed on the appropriate map, and the researcher then need only search one enumeration district rather than an entire ward of the city. Since enumeration districts were not used in 1870, a system was devised in which a systematic sample of individuals was taken from the census. Their addresses were determined by checking the 1870 and 1871 Chicago city directories, and plots were then made on a map using the date each of these persons was enumerated as the key. Using this system, a researcher can determine the most likely date on which an individual would have been enumerated at a particular address. This system also allows researchers to look at the population characteristics of particular neighborhoods or other areas smaller than a ward.[1]

Other Census Sources and Aids

The Newberry Library has ward maps for many cities and detail maps for many counties. See Chapter 2, "Maps, Atlases and Geographical Sources" for further information. The National Archives has produced a microfilm series entitled "Census Descriptions of Geographical Subdivisions and Enumeration Districts." These are written descriptions, not maps, and may be especially useful to researchers wishing to narrow down a search area. The library holds this microfilm series for all states from 1830-80; for Delaware, District of Columbia, Florida, Georgia, Hawaii, Idaho, and Illinois for 1900; and for Georgia, Idaho, and Illinois for 1910.

Besides the census population schedules which record names of individuals, the Newberry also has many census statistical reports and summaries. For instance, the Card Catalogue subject heading "[Name of State].Census" is simply a numerical tally of census data. United States Census Statistical Reports are available through the fifteenth census (1930), and the census summaries are available for the sixteenth through nineteenth censuses (1940-70). A convenient reference source for historical information on population, migration, labor, and social statistics is *Historical Statistics of the United States: Colonial Times to 1970* (1975) published by the U. S. Bureau of the Census.

FEDERAL NON-POPULATION SCHEDULES

Non-population censuses include mortality, agricultural, and manufacturing schedules. The *Guide to Genealogical Research in the National Archives* (1982) provides detailed information on the contents of these non-population schedules. The agricultural schedules include the name of the farm owner or tenant, and details of the farm operation such as crops raised and livestock owned. Mortality schedules record the names and causes of death of those who died during the year previous to 1 June of the census years 1850-80. The manufacturing schedules list the name of the company or owner and record the type and value of materials, labor, and products. The Illinois agricultural and manufacturing schedules for 1850-80 are available on microfilm at the Newberry. Mortality schedules are available on microfilm or as printed transcripts or indexes for many states. They can be located in the Card Catalogue under the state name subject heading, and then under various subdivisions including "Registers of Births, etc.," "Census," and "Genealogy." The "Registers of Births, etc." subdivision includes births, deaths, and marriages, not births only.

STATE AND TERRITORIAL CENSUS SCHEDULES

In addition to the decennial federal population census, a number of states took censuses in the nineteenth and twentieth centuries. Information recorded on state censuses varies. Some, such as Illinois, record only the names of heads of households. Others record even more information than is found in the federal census. In 1885 censuses were taken in five states and territories with federal assistance. The Newberry has the schedules for Colorado, Dakota, and Florida, but not those for Nebraska and New Mexico.

The Newberry holds the following state census schedules:

Colorado:	1885. Includes population, mortality, agricultural, and manufacturing schedules.
Dakota:	1885. Transcribed in *Collections of the State Historical Society of North Dakota,* vol. 4, 1913.
Florida:	1885. Includes population, mortality, agricultural, and manufacturing schedules.
Illinois:	1855, 1865, and remaining fragments from 1825, 1830, 1835, and 1845.
Iowa:	1915 (part).
Nevada:	1875.
New York:	1855 (part), 1875 (part), 1905 (part), and 1925.
Wisconsin:	1905.

NOTES

1. Keith Schlesinger and Peggy Tuck Sinko, "Urban Finding Aid for Manuscript Census Searches," *National Genealogical Society Quarterly* 69 (September 1981): 171-80.

CHAPTER 4

UNITED STATES CHURCH RECORDS AND RELIGIOUS DENOMINATIONS

The Newberry Library has an extensive collection on religious denominations in the United States. A wide variety of works is available from historical studies, minutes and journals of religious conventions, biographical works on clergy and laypersons to histories or records of a single congregation.

Relevant entries in the Card Catalogue are found by checking under the name of the denomination for histories, bibliographies, collective biographies of clergy and prominent laypersons, encyclopedias, theological works, hymnals, and church periodicals and magazines. Denominational names have undergone many changes over the years, and researchers should define as narrowly as possible the denomination in which they are interested. There are several branches of Baptists, Lutherans, and other bodies, and Card Catalogue entries may be found under each separate name. For example, there are entries in the Newberry Card Catalogue under "Lutheran" and "Evangelical Lutheran," "Baptists," "Southern Baptist Convention," "Primitive Baptists," "American Baptists," and "Northern Baptists." Works on a single congregation will have catalogue cards or cross-reference cards under both the name of the church or synagogue and the location. For example, if a researcher wanted to know if the library had anything on the First Presbyterian Church of Wheaton, Illinois, he or she could check the Card Catalogue under either "Wheaton, Illinois, First Presbyterian Church" or "First Presbyterian Church, Wheaton, Illinois."

The library has a good collection of secondary historical works on various denominations, both on the national and state level. Two examples are *History of the Baptists in Vermont* (1913) by Rev. Henry Crocker, and *Hoosier Disciples; A Comprehensive History of the Christian Churches (Disciples of Christ) in Indiana* (1966) by Henry K. Shaw. Encyclopedic works exist for several denominations and are very useful for biographical sketches, discussions of theology, and information on divisions, mergers, and name changes within the denomination. The Newberry has several such encyclopedias including *Encyclopaedia of the Presbyterian Church in the United States of America* (1884); *Centennial Encyclopedia of the African Methodist Episcopal Church...* (1916); and *The Mennonite Encyclopedia,* 4 volumes (1955-59).

The Newberry has extensive holdings of nineteenth century minutes of Congregational and Methodist Episcopal Church conventions in New England and journals of the annual conventions of the Protestant Episcopal Church throughout the United States. These generally contain reports from individual congregations, lists of clergy, and reports on the state of religion. Researchers also have available the *Official Catholic Directory,* which lists churches, schools, orphanages, and other church institutions, from 1897-1971 (a few volumes are missing).

Historical journals or serial publications are available for the following religious bodies: Congregational Church, Jews, Lutherans, Mennonites, Methodists, Moravians, Mormons, Presbyterians, Protestant Episcopal Church, Quakers, Reformed Church, Roman Catholics, and Unitarians. In addition, there are runs of some nineteenth and early twentieth century religious journals and magazines, although many of them are small and incomplete. The library has a good collection of vital records transcribed from religious newspapers and periodicals, including such titles as *Index to Marriage Notices in The Southern Churchman, 1835-1941* (1942), *American Vital Records from the Baptist Register,* 2 volumes (1956-59), and *Marriages and Obituaries from the New Orleans Christian Advocate* (1980). The Historical Records Survey of the Works Progress Administration compiled and printed in the 1930s and 40s many inventories of church archives, directories of churches and religious organizations, and guides to church vital statistics records. These sources should not be overlooked. For more information, see Chapter 2, "Publications of the Works Progress Administration."

Numerous histories of individual congregations are available. Some representative titles are *Centennial Book of the Methodist Episcopal Church, Barton, Vermont* (1928); *The First Colored Baptist Church in North America. Constituted at Savannah, Georgia, January 20, A. D. 1788. With Biographical Sketches of the Pastors* (1888) by James M.

Simms; and John E. Rothensteiner's *Chronicles of an Old Missouri Parish; Historical Sketches of St. Michael's Church, Fredericktown, Madison County, Missouri...* (1928). Such books vary greatly in content. The Newberry also has extensive holdings of transcribed church records, including baptisms, marriages, death and cemetery records, and church minutes. Such works as *Record of the First Baptist Church of Christ in Sardinia, Erie County, New York* (1980) or *The Minutes of the Monthly Meetings of the Middle Run Baptist Church (Predestinarian) July 27, 1799-April 20, 1900* (1973), from Greene County, Ohio, have obvious value for local historians and genealogists, not only because of the vital records they contain, but also because of the information the minutes reveal on the social life and customs of church members and their influence on the community.

Family Bible records present a special problem. The Newberry has a large collection of Bibles, but they are catalogued by language and date of publication, not by owner's name, and there is no list indicating which, if any, of the Bibles contain family records. Many transcripts of family Bible records are found under the family name in the Local and Family History Vertical File. Others, including many compiled by patriotic organizations, are found in the same file under a geographical location. In the Card Catalogue, such compilations are generally listed under a geographical location, which could be a county, state, or even the United States, then under one of two rather broad subdivisions "Genealogy" or "Registers of Births, etc." This method of classification presents problems since a single Bible may contain family records from several different locations.

In addition to all the printed works on churches, synagogues, and religious groups in the greater Chicago area, the Newberry also has microfilms of the original church records of several early area congregations. Microfilmed records are available for the First Presbyterian Church, Wheaton, Illinois (formerly the First Church of Christ), 1866-1980; St. John United Church of Christ, Naperville, Illinois (formerly Evangelical Lutheran Church of St. John the Evangelist), 1860-1942; Evangelical Lutheran Church of St. Luke, Chicago, 1884-1975; and St. James Evangelical Lutheran Church, Chicago, 1870-1951. The library is also due to receive the microfilmed parish registers of all parishes of the Roman Catholic Archdiocese of Chicago founded before 1915. These microfilms will come to the library through the cooperative efforts of the Archdiocese, the Genealogical Society of Utah, and the Council of Northeastern Illinois Genealogical Societies. Many of the registers begin before the Chicago Fire, the earliest being the register of St. Mary's Church beginning in 1833. Records from other denominations are expected, including records of several congregations in North Shore communities.

A number of works at the Newberry deal specifically with genealogy and individual religious bodies. Several how-to-do-it books are available for tracing Jewish ancestry, including Dan Rottenberg's *Finding our Fathers: A Guidebook to Jewish Genealogy* (1977) and Arthur Kurzweil's *From Generation to Generation: How to Trace Your Jewish Genealogy and Family History* (1980). Periodicals which deal exclusively with family history include *Toledot,* the Magazine of Jewish Genealogy, (1977+) and *Mennonite Family History,* (1982+). The library has a very good collection on Quaker genealogy, including several bibliographies, many family histories, transcripts of monthly meeting records, and the seven-volume *Encyclopedia of American Quaker Genealogy* (1936-77), edited by William Wade Hinshaw and later by Willard Heiss.

CHAPTER 5

ETHNIC AND NATIVE AMERICAN SOURCES

Immigrant groups which settled in the U. S. prior to 1900 are well represented in The Newberry Library's holdings. The largest body of material is for Germans, followed by the Irish and Scandinavians. The library has good holdings on Hispanics in the Southwest (Colorado, Utah, Arizona, New Mexico, and Texas) through the first half of the nineteenth century. A small body of Dutch material is available. There is little on the French (except for the period of exploration in the seventeenth and eighteenth centuries), orientals, or Eastern Europeans, with the exception of the Poles, for whom there is some material. Holdings on Italians are rather weak, although the library has acquired many of the recent historical studies on Italian-Americans. Until recently, the Newberry's holdings on Afro-Americans were not distinguished. A large body of material has now been acquired and is described below.

To locate material on ethnic groups, researchers must check several different subject headings in the Card Catalogue. Some examples are:

"Polish-Americans in the U. S."
"Poles in the U. S."
"Poles in Detroit"
"German Americans--Texas"
"Germans in Chicago"

Material on ethnic groups includes historical and newspaper bibliographies, studies of immigrants in a particular city or state, a very fine collection of emigrant guides in foreign languages, and works of a genealogical nature. Historical journals or serial publications are available on Germans, Poles, Swedes, Irish, Danes, Italians, Norwegians, Hispanics, Dutch, and Afro-Americans.

Biographical sketches are found in nineteenth and early twentieth century collective biographies devoted to a particular ethnic group and in works about benevolent and fraternal organizations. Often these works are in foreign languages. A few examples from the Newberry are: *Runristningar: Independent Order of Vikings, 1890-1915* (1915), a register in Swedish; *History of the Friendly Sons of St. Patrick and of the Hibernian Society For the Relief of Emigrants From Ireland* (1892), which contains biographical sketches of members of this Pennsylvania organization; and *Nordmaendene i Amerika, Deres Historie og Rekord* (1907) by Martin Ulvestad, which names hundreds of Norwegian settlers, and lists Norwegians who fought in the Civil War.

In 1986 the library received a generous grant from the Joyce Foundation and embarked on a program to expand holdings relating to Afro-American family history, especially the black family in the South during the antebellum, Civil War, and Reconstruction eras. To date the library has acquired the microfilm series "Records of Ante-Bellum Southern Plantations from the Revolution Through the Civil War," the 1850 and 1860 census slave schedules, various records of the Freedmen's Bureau and the Freedmen's Savings and Trust Company (National Archives microfilm), "Index to Compiled Service Records for the United States Colored Troops," and records concerning fugitive and emancipated slaves in the District of Columbia. More information on the contents of these records is found in Chapter 13, "The South."

GENERAL BIBLIOGRAPHIES AND GUIDES

Wayne Charles Miller, et al. *A Comprehensive Bibliography for the Study of American Minorities,* 1976. A very good guide to English language sources with over 29,000 entries.

Stephan Thernstrom, ed. *Harvard Encyclopedia of American Ethnic Groups,* 1980. Good starting place. Each ethnic group is covered by an essay and bibliography.

German-Americans
Der Deutsche Pionier. 18 vols., 1869-87. A monthly magazine of articles, biographical sketches and obituaries. Published in Cincinnati, but contains information on Germans throughout the United States.

Michael Keresztesi and Gary R. Cocozzoli. *German-American History and Life: A Guide to Information Sources,* 1980. Annotated.

Emil Meynen. *Bibliography on German Settlements in Colonial North America, Especially on the Pennsylvania Germans and their Descendants, 1683-1933,* 1937. The library has a large collection on the Pennsylvania Germans. See Chapter 12, "Pennsylvania."

Henry August Pochmann. *Bibliography of German Culture in America to 1940.* Rev. and corr., 1982. Contains 18,500 entries. Not annotated.

Clifford Neal Smith and Anna Piszczan-Czaja Smith. *American Genealogical Resources in German Archives,* 1977.

_____. *Encyclopedia of German-American Genealogical Research,* 1976.

_____. German-American Genealogical Research Monograph Series, 1973+.

Don Heinrich Tolzmann. *German-Americana: A Bibliography,* 1975. Continues Pochmann; most entries are from 1941-73. No annotations.

Irish-Americans
Seamus P. Metress. *The Irish-American Experience: A Guide to the Literature,* 1981. Not annotated.

Scandinavian-Americans
Enok Mortensen. *Danish-American Life and Letters: A Bibliography,* 1945, repr. 1979. Not annotated.

Polish-Americans
Thaddeus J. Obal. *A Bibliography for Genealogical Research Involving Polish Ancestry,* 1978.

Joseph W. Zurawski. *Polish American History and Culture: A Classified Bibliography,* 1975.

Hispanic-Americans
Henry Putney Beers. *Spanish and Mexican Records of the American Southwest,* 1979.

Lyman De Platt, "Hispanic-American Records and Research." In *Ethnic Genealogy: A Research Guide,* ed. by Jessie Carney Smith, 1983. Useful introduction with bibliography.

Matt S. Meier. *Bibliography of Mexican American History,* 1984. Good.

Dutch-Americans

Elton J. Bruins. *The Dutch in America: A Bibliographical Guide for Students,* 1975.

Linda Pegman Doezema. *Dutch Americans: A Guide to Information Sources,* 1979. Annotated.

Italian-Americans

Francesco Cordasco. *Italian Americans: A Guide to Information Sources,* 1978. Annotated.

Afro-Americans

Material on Afro-Americans is voluminous. Listed below are only a few works to introduce researchers to the subject:

James de T. Abajian. *Blacks in Selected Newspapers, Censuses and Other Sources; an Index to Names and Subjects,* 1977.

Charles L. Blockson, "Black American Records and Research." In *Ethnic Genealogy: A Research Guide,* ed. by Jessie Carney Smith, 1983. A thorough discussion with excellent bibliography.

Charles L. Blockson. *Black Genealogy,* 1977.

Richard Newman. *Black Access: A Bibliography of Afro-American Bibliographies,* 1984.

Dwight L. Smith. *Afro-American History: A Bibliography.* 2 vols., 1974-81. Covers periodical literature from 1954-1978.

Southern Workman, 1872-1939. Official monthly journal of Hampton Institute in Virginia, a school open to American Indians and Afro-Americans.

David H. Streets. *Slave Genealogy: A Research Guide with Case Studies,* 1986.

James D. Walker. *Black Genealogy: How to Begin,* 1977. Good.

AMERICAN INDIAN GENEALOGICAL RESEARCH

The Newberry Library is known throughout the country for both its genealogy and American Indian collections. Consequently, researchers interested in American Indian genealogy will find a wealth of relevant material. The library's holdings on Indians and Indian/non-Indian relations are among the best in the United States. This chapter cannot describe fully the American Indian collection at the Newberry, but can merely direct the researcher to some of the most useful sources related to Indian genealogical research.

American Indian genealogical research is not a simple matter, but it is also not impossible. Researchers must, however, be able to identify the tribal group to which an ancestor belonged in order to have hope of success. Other factors to consider are the status of mixed bloods and the fact that many records may be dispersed geographically throughout the country among different agencies, bureaus, archives, and other repositories. Much material needed by researchers interested in Indian genealogy is not in print, but will be found in the National Archives, the Bureau of Indian Affairs, the Bureau of American Ethnology, and tribal offices. While this material will not be found at the Newberry, the library does have an extensive collection of guides and inventories, particularly for Indian materials at the National Archives. In the Newberry Card Catalogue, one can check under the names of individual tribes and under the more general subject heading "Indians of North America." The greatest amount of information is available for the Five Civilized Tribes.

Much useful material on Indian genealogy has appeared in journals such as the *Oklahoma Genealogical Society Quarterly* (1955+), and *The Journal of American Indian Family Research* (1980+). Some other useful sources include a series on Cherokee cemeteries, *Our People and Where They Rest* (1969+) by James W. Tyner and Alice Tyner Timmons, and the eight-volume *Biographical and Historical Index of American Indians and Persons Involved in Indian Affairs* (1966) from the U. S. Department of the Interior Library.

A great many compilations, transcriptions, and microfilm copies of Indian censuses and emigration rolls are available, mostly for the nineteenth century and for the Five Civilized Tribes. These can be identified in several of the bibliographies listed below. Nearly all the printed compilations will be found at the library. In addition, the Newberry has 299 of 692 microfilm reels of the Indian Census Rolls, 1885-1940, for reservation Indians. The Oklahoma Genealogical Society has published *A Compilation of Records from the Choctaw Nation, Indian Territory* (1976), which includes the 1896 Choctaw Nation Census, cemetery, church, and marriage records, plus other miscellaneous information. A great deal of material will also be found on church missions to the Indians.

Other sources that should not be overlooked are Indian newspapers and publications from Indian schools. The Newberry has the *Cherokee Phoenix* (February 1828-May 1834); papers and publications from the U. S. Indian School at Carlisle, Pennsylvania; *The Indian Leader,* 1933 (vol. 37) to date, from the Haskell Institute, Lawrence, Kansas; and *The Indian School Journal,* volumes 7-25 (1907-25), from the U. S. Indian

School at Chilocco, Oklahoma. Some abstracts of Indian vital records from newspapers are also available.

The library has a great deal of material on the Indian Rights Association, organized in Philadelphia in 1882. This includes the "Papers of the Indian Rights Association," covering the years 1882 to 1968. The "Papers," which are on microfilm, contain much correspondence with Indians and are well indexed. The "John Collier Papers, 1922-1968," from the Yale University Library, are also available on microfilm. Collier was Commissioner of Indian Affairs and an Indian rights activist.

Bibliographies And Guides

Dictionary Catalogue of the Edward E. Ayer Collection of Americana and American Indians in The Newberry Library. 16 vols., plus supplements, 1961-80.

Bob Blankenship. *Cherokee Roots,* 1978.

Cecelia S. Carpenter. *How to Research American Indian Blood Lines: A Manual on Indian Genealogical Research,* 1984.

Dick Clark. *Cherokee Ancestor Research,* 1979.

Frederick W. Hodge. *Handbook of American Indians North of Mexico,* 1907-10, repr. 1969. Useful for the regularization of tribal names.

E. Kay Kirkham. *Our Native Americans, Their Records of Genealogical Value,* 1980. Very good. Has a guide to the Indian Census Rolls and useful bibliographies.

George Peter Murdock. *Ethnographic Bibliography of North America.* 5 vols., 4th ed., 1975.

George J. Nixon. "Records Relating to Native American Research: The Five Civilized Tribes." In *The Source,* edited by Arlene Eakle and Johni Cerny, 1984. Has a lengthy bibliography of printed sources, nearly all of which are at the Newberry.

Jimmy B. Parker. "American Indian Records and Research." In *Ethnic Genealogy,* edited by Jessie Carney Smith, 1983. Good, with helpful illustrations.

Francis Paul Prucha. *A Bibliographical Guide to the History of Indian-White Relations in the United States,* 1977 plus 1982 supplement.

James P. Ronda and James Axtell. *Indian Missions: A Critical Bibliography,* 1978.

Smithsonian Institution. *Handbook of North American Indians,* 1978+.
Projected twenty volume set. Very important.

John R. Swanton. *The Indian Tribes of North America,* 1952. Good for
identifying village names and for the spelling of village and tribal
names.

CHAPTER 6

MILITARY GROUPS AND THEIR RECORDS

Records containing information on military service and veterans' benefits for individual soldiers and their dependents can be very valuable to genealogists and local historians. There are a large number of card catalogue subject headings at the Newberry which one may consult for information on military service. One approach is to check "U.S.-History--[Name of War]--" and then further subdivisions such as "Biography," "Cemeteries," "Regimental Histories," "Rosters," and "Registers." One can also check names of individual states, then subdivisions such as "Militia," "Adjutant General," "Infantry," "Cavalry," and "History--[Name of War]." Lists of pensioners will be found in the Card Catalogue under "Pensions, Military."

GENERAL WORKS

Lists of officers in the regular Army and Navy have been published by Francis B. Heitman, Thomas H. S. Hamersly, and William H. Powell. The library has these lists, as well as the *Official Army Register* for 1784-92, and 1813-1968, which lists all officers of the regular Army. The *Navy Register*, which again lists only officers, is available for 1825-1967 (a few volumes are missing). The *Navy Directory* and the *Army List and Directory* are both available for the years 1923-41. In addition, there are some registers of Reserve officers and lists of cadets and graduates of the service academies at West Point and Annapolis.

Many helpful references on Naval personnel are found in Myron J. Smith, Jr.'s American Naval Bibliography Series. The four volumes in the series are *Navies in the American Revolution: A Bibliography* (1973), *The American Navy, 1789-1860* (1974), *American Civil War Navies* (1972), and *The American Navy, 1865-1918* (1974). Lists of those granted bounty land warrants by the federal government and the state of Virginia, in the U.S. Military District of Ohio and the Virginia Military District of Ohio, plus all Federal Bounty Land Warrants for Revolutionary War service, appear in the *Federal Land Series,* 4 volumes (1972-82) by Clifford Neal Smith.

COLONIAL WARS AND THE
REVOLUTIONARY WAR

There is no comprehensive index or list of those who served during the various colonial wars, and many records of military service are no longer extant. Many of the rosters and muster rolls that have survived contain little or no personal information beyond the name of the soldier. Published lists of colonial soldiers and militiamen do exist for a number of states including Connecticut, Massachusetts, New Hampshire, New York, Pennsylvania, and Rhode Island. For colonial soldiers in the South, see Murtie June Clark's *Colonial Soldiers of the South, 1732-1774* (1983), which consists primarily of information taken from muster rolls and payrolls for militias in Maryland, Virginia, the Carolinas, and Georgia. Approximately 55,000 soldiers are included. Works on King Philip's War are found in the Card Catalogue under the heading "King Philip's War," while the other colonial wars are found under the heading "U.S.--History--[Name of War]."

Information is more plentiful on soldiers in the American Revolution. There are several very fine guides and bibliographies which alert researchers to the many published sources on military records and veterans' benefits. *Locating Your Revolutionary War Ancestor* (1983) by James C. and Lila L. Neagles, has a very good bibliography of printed lists, rosters, muster rolls, and other sources, plus a good synopsis of changes in military benefit laws. Two other good sources are *Fighters for Independence: A Guide to Sources of Biographical Information on Soldiers and Sailors of the American Revolution* (1977) by J. Todd White and Charles H. Lesser, and George K. Schweitzer's *Revolutionary War Genealogy* (1982). A fourth important source is *Revolutionary America, 1763-1789: A Bibliography,* 2 volumes (1984) compiled by Ronald M. Gephart. This outstanding, annotated work treats all aspects of the Revolution in great detail and has several sections that deal with individuals, including a large biographical section and much on troops and soldiers at the state and local level. Both periodical articles and books are included.

As is the case with the colonial wars, no comprehensive list of all Revolutionary War soldiers exists, but there is at least one publication (usually more) for each state involved in the Revolution, as well as for those states where Revolutionary War veterans later settled. Researchers should remember that soldiers may have been members of local militia units, "state" lines, or the Continental Line, and many people served in more than one type of unit. This often explains why a soldier is listed in one publication on a given state, but not in others. Publications in the Newberry collection include rosters, muster rolls, compiled service records, pension lists, and applicants for pensions, works on veterans buried in a given state, and lists of bounty land warrants issued.

One good list, although far from complete, of Revolutionary soldiers and those who did patriotic service, is the *DAR Patriotic Index,* 2 volumes (1966-79, plus 1982 supplement), which includes only those soldiers and patriots having a descendant who joined the Daughters of the American Revolution. The National Genealogical Society has published *Index to Revolutionary War Pension Applications* (1976), an index to those records found at the National Archives. Some states also granted pensions and bounty lands to Revolutionary War soldiers, and some of these records have been published in works such as *Virginia Revolutionary War State Pensions* (1980) by the Virginia Genealogical Society and *North Carolina Land Grants in Tennessee, 1778-1791* (1958) by Betty G. C. Cartwright and Lillian Johnson Gardiner.

Several volumes exist that identify foreign troops who fought on both sides of the Revolutionary struggle. French participants appear in *Les Combattants Francais de la Guerre Americaine, 1778-83* (1905). Clifford Neal Smith has published a number of volumes on British soldiers and German mercenaries who remained in the United States, all of which are at the Newberry. Another series on German mercenaries is *Hessische Truppen im Amerikanischen Unabhängigkeitskrieg* (1972+).

WAR OF 1812

The library does have on microfilm the *Index to Compiled Service Records of the War of 1812* from the National Archives, but not the service records themselves. A good bibliography of published material on War of 1812 military personnel is found in George K. Schweitzer's *War of 1812 Genealogy* (1983). Published lists of troops exist for most states and are part of the Newberry collection. Bounty land warrants for the War of 1812 were issued for land in Illinois, Missouri, and Arkansas. The list of warranties for Illinois land is found in *War of 1812 Bounty Lands in Illinois* (1977), reprinted with an index from the *U. S. Serial Set.*

MEXICAN WAR

Norman E. Tutorow's *The Mexican-American War: An Annotated Bibliography* (1981), will be helpful to those seeking information on individuals serving in the Mexican War. Tutorow's sections on military units are informative and include references to books, articles, manuscripts, and government documents. The Newberry does have a very good collection of books and articles on Mexican War troops. For a list of officers of that war see William Hugh Robarts' *Mexican War Veterans. A Complete Roster of the Regular and Volunteer Troops in the War Between the United States and Mexico, From 1846 to 1848* (1887).

CIVIL WAR

More has been written about the American Civil War than any other military conflict in which the United States has been involved, and The Newberry Library has a very large selection of these writings. Among the many guides and bibliographies which have been written, there are several which contain information on individuals or specific military units. The most important is *Military Bibliography of the Civil War*, 3 volumes (1961-72) by Charles E. Dornbusch. This is an excellent guide to regimental histories, personal narratives, diaries, and published letters, appearing in both books and periodicals. Researchers will find an excellent collection of Civil War regimental histories at the library. Frederick H. Dyer's *A Compendium of the War of the Rebellion* (1908) provides additional information on Union Army troops. Dyer lists troops assigned to each command, troops engaged in each individual battle, along with brief regimental histories. A work similar to Dornbusch, but for the Navy, is Myron J. Smith, Jr.'s *American Civil War Navies* (1972). *Civil War Books: A Critical Bibliography*, 2 volumes (1967-69) by Allan Nevins, James I. Robertson, Jr., and Bell I. Wiley, briefly reviews about five thousand books on the Civil War. A large number of these are regimental histories and personal narratives. *Tracing Your Civil War Ancestor* (1973) by Bertram H. Groene is a basic, but good guide to the subject. George K. Schweitzer's *Civil War Genealogy* (1980) is a useful source with good bibliographies.

Most states, both North and South, have published lists of all soldiers who served in volunteer regiments raised in the state. Many were published shortly after the Civil War by the state Adjutant General's office, and some appeared to commemorate the Civil War Centennial one hundred years later. These are excellent sources of information on military units and individuals; however, many are not arranged in alphabetical order by individual soldier or do not have alphabetical indexes, although indexes are increasingly becoming available. A number of them are at present simply arranged by regiment and then by company. In addition to these printed rosters of state troops, the library also has on microfilm from the National Archives the "Index to Compiled Service Records of Volunteer Union Soldiers who Served in Organizations from the State of Illinois," and "Index to Compiled Service Records for the United States Colored Troops."

Two large compilations, both indexed, are often ignored by researchers, but are worth consulting. *The War of the Rebellion: A Compilation of the Official Records of the Union and Confederate Armies* (1880-1901) consists of seventy volumes of selected official records. Although few enlisted men are mentioned by name, unless they did something noteworthy, one can learn about the movements of military units and the skirmishes and battles in which they participated. An atlas accompanies this set and is useful in local and family history research. See Chapter 2 for more information. The companion set to the above compilation is *Official Records of the Union and Confederate Navies in the War of the Rebellion* (1894-1922) in thirty-one volumes.

There are several sources of information on those who died while in military service. Among these are lists of those dying in prison camps, in the North and South and lists of those buried in military cemeteries. One of the largest lists of Civil War dead is *Roll of Honor. Names of Soldiers who Died in Defence* [sic] *of the American Union, Interred in the National Cemeteries* (1865-71), issued in twenty-seven parts by the U. S. Quartermaster's Department.

Some lists of federal Civil War pensioners exist, although there is no published index to Civil War pension applications. Several southern states issued pensions to Civil War veterans, and a number of these lists have been published, for example, *Index to Applications for Texas Confederate Pensions* (1975) compiled by John M. Kinney. Some southern states also compiled information on, and conducted censuses of Confederate veterans long after the end of the war. Two examples, which contain much personal information, are *The Tennessee Civil War Veterans Questionnaires,* 5 volumes (1985), compiled by Gustavus W. Dyer and John Trotwood Moore, which includes all known Tennessee Civil War veterans in 1914, 1915, and 1920, and *Arkansas 1911 Census of Confederate Veterans,* 3 volumes (1977), edited by Bobbie J. McLane and Capitola Glazner. Another possible source of information on Confederate veterans is the magazine *The Confederate Veteran,* which appeared in forty volumes from 1893 to 1932. A complete run of this magazine, plus an index, is at the Newberry. In 1890 the federal government took a census of Union veterans and widows. Records of the states A to I (except for District of Columbia) were lost in a fire in Washington, D.C., in 1921. The Newberry has records of some of the remaining states either on microfilm or in transcription form.

One more final source may be helpful, although it does not deal directly with soldiers. Gary B. Mills compiled *Civil War Claims in the South: An Index of Civil War Damage Claims Filed Before the Southern*

Claims Commission, 1871-1880 (1980). Over 22,000 damage claims were filed before this Commission, whose records are in the National Archives.

LOYALISTS

During the American Revolution, a number of American colonists remained loyal to Great Britain. Many of these Loyalists fled the United States during and after the Revolution. The Newberry Library has extensive material on both the Loyalists in the United States and those in exile in Canada, Great Britain, Florida, and the West Indies. Works on the Loyalists are found in the Card Catalogue under the subject headings "American Loyalists" and "United Empire Loyalists" (for those who moved to Canada).

The best bibliographic source on the Loyalists is *Revolutionary America, 1763-1789: A Bibliography,* 2 volumes (1984), compiled by Ronald M. Gephart. Gephart's excellent annotated compilation includes primary and secondary books, maps, manuscripts, periodical articles, and dissertations. The bibliography has a section on Loyalist troops and an entire chapter entitled "The Loyalists in America and in Exile." Another important bibliography is *A Bibliography of Loyalist Source Material in the United States, Canada, and Great Britain* (1981) edited by Gregory Palmer. This work concentrates on manuscript material and Loyalist newspapers, although there are some entries for primary printed sources.

The Newberry holds a number of rare works including *The Particular Case of the Georgia Loyalists: In Addition to the General Case and Claim of the American Loyalists,...* (1783); *The Case and Claim of the American Loyalists Impartially Stated and Considered* (1783); Joseph Galloway's *The Claim of the American Loyalists Reviewed and Maintained Upon Incontrovertible Principles of Law and Justice* (1788); and *Black List. A List of Those Tories who Took Part With Great-Britain, in the Revolutionary War, and Were Attainted of High Treason. Commonly Called the Black List!* (1802).

Many rosters and muster rolls of Loyalist troops have been published (often as periodical articles) and are found in the Newberry's collection. One important compilation is Murtie June Clark's *Loyalists in the Southern Campaign of the Revolutionary War,* 3 volumes (1981). Clark searched muster rolls, payrolls, petitions, and vouchers of Loyalist troops and has included not only troops from the South, but also some from the Mid-Atlantic colonies who fought in the South. Some information also appears on Loyalist refugees, prisoners, and sympathizers. This work includes approximately 35,000 entries. The Newberry has a very fine collection of Revolutionary War pamphlets, about half of which are British publications, and many of which deal with the Loyalists. In 1922 Ruth Lapham prepared a check list of the 574 pamphlets then in the Newberry collection--*Check List of American Revolutionary War Pamphlets in The Newberry Library.*

Names of individual Loyalists appear in several published lists. One of the best known is Lorenzo Sabine's *Biographical Sketches of Loyalists of the American Revolution,* published in two editions in 1847 and 1864. A revised and enlarged edition, edited by Gregory Palmer, appeared in 1984. Peter Wilson Coldham's *American Loyalist Claims* (1980) consists of information taken from the records of the Loyalist Claim Commission in the British Public Records Office and overlaps heavily with the revised edition of Sabine.

There are several important compilations on the United Empire Loyalists. The first is *The Centennial of the Settlement of Upper Canada by the United Empire Loyalists, 1784-1884* (1885), which includes a copy of the "Old Empire Loyalists List," the official list of those who came to Canada through 1798. Despite the title, this is not entirely a list of Loyalists, but also includes some settlers and discharged British soldiers. This book has been reprinted as *The Old United Empire Loyalists List* (1969). Another important source is "United Empire Loyalists. Enquiry Into Losses and Services in Consequence of Their Loyalty," a record of the 1400 claims heard by the Commissioners of the Loyalist Claim Commission who were sent to Canada. This report appears in *Second Report of the Bureau of Archives for the Province of Ontario* for 1904. Recently, the United Empire Loyalists' Association of Canada, Toronto Branch, published *Loyalist Lineages of Canada, 1783-1983* (1984). Lineages of over 1300 members from throughout Canada appear. A final source is *Annual Transactions of the United Empire Loyalists' Association of Ontario,* volumes 3-8 (1899/1900-1917/26), which contains historical articles and biographical sketches of Loyalists in Ontario.

CHAPTER 7

HERALDRY, NOBILITY, AND HEREDITARY SOCIETIES

Works on heraldry and the noble houses and families of Europe form a very large and significant collection at The Newberry Library. Although armorials--collections of pictures of coats of arms--generally come first to mind when one thinks of heraldry books, works on heraldry in the Newberry collection cover a wide variety of subjects in many different languages. In addition to armorials which allow one to find a coat of arms associated with a particular surname, there are also ordinaries of arms which work from the description of the arms to a surname. At the library one can find books on mottoes, crests, civic and ecclesiastical heraldry, as well as numerous guides, handbooks, and grammars for understanding heraldry.

Heraldry is a very complex subject, and its rules and laws vary from country to country. Many, if not most, Americans are misinformed or ignorant of the proper use and meaning of a coat of arms. A good, brief introduction to the subject can be found in Jean Stephenson's *Heraldry for the American Genealogist* (1959). The heraldry collection at the Newberry serves the needs of many researchers besides family historians. Coats of arms can be found on a variety of objects--pieces of silver, paintings and portraits, bookplates--and the identification of the coat of arms is often crucial in helping establish the provenance of an object.

To assist Newberry researchers looking for pictures of coats of arms, the Library has a Heraldry Card File Index. This file, located in the Reference and Bibliographical Center, was compiled over many years by Joseph C. Wolf, former Custodian of the Local and Family History Section. Wolf's Index contains approximately 75,000 references to pictures of coats of arms found in numerous Newberry books. Most of the entries are for surnames, but some references to civic or ecclesiastical arms also appear. See Chapter 9 for further information on the Heraldry File. A similar index compiled at the St. Louis Public Library has been published, and this *Heraldry Index of the St. Louis Public Library* (1980) can also prove useful in locating pictures of coats of arms.

The Newberry's works on heraldry and noble families cover all the countries of Western Europe, although the collection is strongest for Great Britain. Chronologically the collection includes several sixteenth century books and manuscripts, as well as recently published works in the field. The earliest manuscript armorial at the library is Robert Cook's "Armorial Bearings of the Kings and Noble Families of Great Britain from the Reign of William the Conqueror to that of James I." This manuscript of coats of arms in color was done in 1572. Some other important and rare items at the library include the 1562 first edition of *The Accedens of Armory* by Gerard Legh; Randle Holme's *The Academy of Armory* (1688); the second edition (1597) of *Workes of Armorie Devided into Three Bookes...* by John Bossewell; five editions of John Guillim's *A Display of Heraldry* (first Newberry edition, 1611); Alexander Nisbet's *A System of Heraldry* (1816); the second edition (1628) of *Le Blason des Armoiries* by Jerome de Bara, and William Berry's *Encyclopaedia Heraldica* (1828-40), which includes the scarce fourth volume.

Below are several bibliographies that will aid researchers.

SELECTED WORKS

P. William Filby. *American and British Genealogy and Heraldry: A Selected List of Books.* 3rd ed., 1983.

Otto Forst-Battaglia. *Traite de Genealogie,* 1949. Good for noble and royal houses of Europe.

George Gatfield. *Guide to Printed Books and Manuscripts Relating to English and Foreign Heraldry and Genealogy,* 1892.

Eckhart Henning and Gabriele Jochums. *Bibliographie Zur Heraldik: Schrifttum Deutschlands und Österreichs bis 1980,* 1984. Covers Germany and Austria.

Thomas Moule. *Bibliotheca Heraldica Magnae Britanniae,* 1822.

Most armorials deal with coats of arms in a specific geographical area. There is no master guide or index to every coat of arms from every country recognizing their use. Below are listed some of the best armorials and encyclopedic works. Publication dates are for the standard edition in use. In many cases, the library will have other editions as well.

Western Europe
J. B. Rietstap. *Armorial General,* 1950 and 1955. The seven-volume *Dictionnaire des Figures Heraldiques* (1894-1903), plus supplements (1926-54), by Theodore de Renesse serves as an ordinary of arms for Rietstap.

Germany and Western Europe
Johann Sibmacher. *Grosses und Allgemeines Wappenbuch.* 82 vols., 1856-1938.

France
Louis P. and A. M. d'Hozier. *Armorial General de la France.* 7 vols., 1865-73.

Henri Jougla de Morenas. *Grand Armorial de France.* 6 vols., 1934-49.

Great Britain
John Bernard Burke. *The General Armory of England, Scotland, Ireland and Wales,* 1884, repr. 1976. Contains no illustrations, but descriptions only.

John W. Papworth. *Ordinary of British Armorials,* 1874, repr. 1977. An ordinary of arms for Burke's *General Armory.*

Italy
Vittorio Spreti. *Enciclopedia Storico-Nobiliare Italiana.* 6 vols. plus appendices, 1928-35.

Poland
Kasper Niesecki. *Herbarz Polski.* 10 vols., 1839-1946, repr. 1979.

Spain and Mexico
Alberto and Arturo Garcia-Caraffa. *Enciclopedia Heraldica y Genealogica Hispano-Americana.* 88 vols., 1919-63.

In addition to works on heraldry, The Newberry Library has an extensive collection on noble houses and families, orders of knighthood, the peerage and baronetage, and military orders. For Great Britain this includes nearly all the published visitations by the heralds, all the Harleian Society publications, and the visitations published by Joseph J. Howard and Frederick A. Crisp, *Visitation of England and Wales,* 21 volumes (1893-1921), and *Visitation of Ireland,* 6 volumes (1897-1918). *Miscellanea Genealogica et Heraldica,* a series of thirty-one volumes published between 1868 and 1938, covers many aspects of British genealogy, heraldry and local history. All standard works on the peerage, baronetage and knighthood can be found at the library. Burke's, Collin's, Dod's, and Debrett's peerages are available, as well as Vicary Gibbs' and George E. Cokayne's *The Complete Peerage,* new edition, 13 volumes (1910-59); *The Scots Peerage,* 9 volumes (1904-14) by Sir James Balfour Paul; and William Betham's *The Baronetage of England,* 4 volumes (1801-04).

The *Almanach de Gotha* is one of the best known and most heavily consulted works on the European nobility. The Newberry lacks only the first three volumes of this work, which appeared annually from 1764 to 1944. Much of the information in the *Almanach* is continued in *Genealogisches Handbuch des Adels,* which first appeared in 1951. Serial works and multi-volume sets on noble families exist for most European countries. Some of those found at the Newberry are listed below:

Austria

Karl Friedrich von Frank. *Standeserhebungen und Gnadenakte für das Deutsche Reiche und die Österreichischen Erblande bis 1806, Sowie Kaiserlich Österreichische bis 1823 mit Einigen Nachträgen Zum Alt-Österreichischen Adels-Lexikon, 1823-1918.* 5 vols., 1967-74.

Constantin von Wurzbach. *Biographisches Lexikon des Kaiserthums Österreich....* 60 vols., 1856-91, repr. 1966-73.

France

Anselme de Sainte-Marie. *Histoire Genealogique et Chronologique de la Maison Royale de France....* 3rd ed., 9 vols., 1726-33.

Francois-Alexandre Aubert de la Chesnaye-Desbois et Badier. *Dictionnaire de la Noblesse, Contenant les Genealogies...,* 1863-76.
Annuaire de la Noblesse Francaise, 1843 to date.
L. DeMagny. *Nobiliaire Universel de France,* 1854-1900.

Germany

Genealogisches Taschenbuch der Adeligen Häuser. Vols.14-19, 1889-94.

Gothaischer Genealogischer Hofkalender. 17 scattered vols., 1797, 1818, 1871-1907.

Gothaisches Genealogisches Taschenbuch der Adeligen Häuser. 38 vols., 1900-39.

Gothaisches Genealogishes Taschenbuch der Freiherrlichen   Häuser. Vols. 39-89, 92, 1889-1939, 1942.

Gothaisches Genealogisches Taschenbuch der Gräflichen Hauser. Vols. 62-112, 1889-1939.

Italy
Libro d'Oro Della Nobilita Italiana, 1910 to date.

Pompeo Litta. *Famiglie Celebri di Italiane.* 13 vols., 1819-52, plus 2nd series, 3 vols., 1902-03.

Netherlands
Nederland's Patriciaat, 1910 to date.

Nederland's Adelsboek, 1903-30.

Russia
Nicolas Ikonnikov. *La Noblesse de Russie.* 11 vols., 1933-40.

Spain
Francisco Fernandez de Bethencourt. *Historia Genealogica y Heraldica de la Monarquia Española.* 9 vols. (The Newberry lacks volume 10), 1897-1920.

Sweden
Sveriges Ridderskaps Och Adels Kalendar, 1882 to date.

Switzerland
Schweizerisches Geschlechterbuch, 1905 to date.

JOURNALS

Archiv für Stamm- und Wappenkunde, 1900-20.

Archivum Heraldicum (formerly *Schweizer Archiv für Heraldik*), 1887-1975.

The Armorial, 1959-69.

The Augustan, 1973 to date.

Coat-Armour. 5 vols., 1971-72. Continued by *The Augustan.*

The Coat of Arms (Heraldry Society of Britain), 1950 to date.

Family History (Institute of Heraldic and Genealogical Studies in England), 1962 to date.

Giornale Araldico-Genealogico-Diplomatico (Italy), 1873-96.

The Herald and Genealogist, 1863-74.

Heraldry in Canada (Heraldry Society of Canada), 1966 to date.

Hidalguia (Spain), 1953 to date.

Bulletin de la Societe Heraldique et Genealogique de France, 1879-98.

PATRIOTIC AND HEREDITARY SOCIETIES

Membership in most patriotic and hereditary societies is based on an ancestor's military service, his or her having been a member of a certain trade or profession, or having been a pioneer settler in a certain area. Family history researchers will find the records and publications of these societies helpful, even if they are not eligible for membership.

Many of these publications contain information on many families and individuals other than just members' ancestors. Some examples are books on Revolutionary War soldiers who lived or are buried in an area, compiled by chapters of the National Society, Daughters of the American Revolution (DAR) and the publications series produced by the Society of Colonial Wars in Rhode Island, which contains facsimiles and transcripts of colonial documents, letters, and diaries.

To obtain information on patriotic and hereditary societies, researchers should consult *The Hereditary Register of the United States of America.* This volume, which is regularly updated, lists each society, provides information on its founding, the requirements for membership, and the name and address of a contact person. The book also includes a list of family associations, although it is not complete.

The Newberry Library has a large and varied collection of material produced by patriotic and hereditary societies. Some of the types of material that can be found include rosters of soldiers, lineages of members, historical and genealogical publications, lists of members' ancestors, directories of members, annual reports, histories of the societies, yearbooks, minutes of annual meetings, and magazines and bulletins. Not all of these sources exist for every society. The library's holdings include a great deal on such large, well-known organizations as the DAR, the Society of Mayflower Descendants, and the Society of Colonial Wars, as well as material on many of the smaller and lesser-known organizations such as the Society of California Pioneers, Descendants of the Illegitimate Sons and Daughters of the Kings of Britain (known as the Royal Bastards), and the Society of the Descendants of the Colonial Clergy.

Listed on the following pages are some of the societies for which the Newberry has large or significant holdings:

National Society, Daughters of the American Revolution

Holdings include the 166-volume *Lineage Book* series; over 100 volumes of Grandparent Papers from Illinois DAR chapters; compilations of genealogical material contributed by Illinois chapters, known as the "Blue Books" (these begin in the late 1930s); annual reports; the *Daughters of the American Revolution Magazine* (1892+); the *DAR Patriot Index*, 2 volumes (1966-79, plus 1982 supplement); and numerous publications and genealogical compilations by chapters from across the country.

General Society of Mayflower Descendants

Holdings include *Mayflower Quarterly* (1935+); *The Mayflower Descendant* (1899-1937, 1985+), published by the Massachusetts Society of Mayflower Descendants; *Mayflower Index* (rev. ed., 1960); and *Mayflower Families Through Five Generations* (1975+), a very important series on the genealogy of early Pilgrim families.

Sons of the American Revolution, Illinois Society

The library has membership applications on microfilm, beginning in 1893, and *The Minute Man*, volumes 6-71 (1916-81), the bulletin of the Illinois society.

National Society, Daughters of the American Colonists

Holdings include over twenty volumes of lineage books and colonial and genealogical records gathered by local chapters. Since about 1980 local chapters of the DAC have regularly sent copies of these genealogical compilations to the Newberry. Some earlier compilations are also held. Some of the material is catalogued, and some can be found in the Local and Family History Vertical File.

Society of Colonial Wars

Holdings include various indexes of ancestors, rolls of members, and registers and rosters for the national organization and many state organizations. Also available are over fifty volumes in the Publications Series of the Society of Colonial Wars in Rhode Island.

National Society of the Colonial Dames of America

The library has, on microfilm, membership applications of individuals living in Illinois. The Colonial Dames have also sponsored the publication of numerous historical works.

National Society, Daughters of Founders and Patriots of America

The library has the Society's *Lineage Books* which presently number thirty-seven volumes.

United Daughters of the Confederacy

Holdings include *The United Daughters of the Confederacy Magazine,* 1940 (vol. 3) to date, and thirteen scattered volumes of annual convention minutes for 1942-69.

Society of Indiana Pioneers

The library has the *Society of Indiana Pioneers Yearbook* (1921 +).

CHAPTER 8

PASSENGER LISTS AND NATURALIZATION RECORDS

T he Newberry Library has a large collection of printed passenger lists
and naturalization records. The library does not, however, have
either the National Archives's passenger arrival lists on microfilm, or the
departure records from Hamburg, Germany. A handout entitled "Passenger Lists," which briefly describes the Newberry's holdings, is available.

PASSENGER LISTS

Information found on passenger lists varies and is frequently of limited
use. It is often extremely difficult, for example, to match positively a
name on a passenger list with the person of that name about whom one
seeks information. Two categories of records are available: records of
passenger arrivals in America, and records of emigrants departing from
Europe.

The first source researchers should consult is *Passenger and Immigration Lists Index* (1981) compiled by P. William Filby and Mary
Keysor Meyer. This index, plus supplements, lists over 700,000 persons
mentioned in *printed* sources. Its companion volume is P. William
Filby's *Passenger and Immigration Lists Bibliography* (1981). The library
has nearly all the works cited in this bibliography. Most printed pas-

senger list compilations cover the pre-1820 period before the U. S. government took responsibility for recording incoming passengers. Many of the lists have appeared in periodicals, and the two works cited above provide the best access to this material. Increasingly, however, compilations are appearing for the post-1820 period, covering either all arrivals at a port for a certain time period, or arrivals by a particular ethnic group. A few of the more important ones are:

Leo Baca. *Czech Immigration Passenger Lists,* 1983. Includes some information taken from newspapers.

Elizabeth P. Bentley. *Passenger Arrivals at the Port of Baltimore, 1820-1834,* 1982.

Galveston County Genealogical Society. *Ships Passenger Lists: Port of Galveston, Texas, 1846-1871,* 1984.

Ira A. Glazier, ed. *The Famine Immigrants: Lists of Irish Immigrants Arriving at the Port of New York, 1846-1851,* 1983+.

Nils William Olsson. *Swedish Passenger Arrivals in U. S. Ports, 1820-1850 (Except New York),* 1979, and *Swedish Passenger Arrivals in New York, 1820-1850,* 1967.

Robert P. Swierenga. *Dutch Immigrants in U. S. Ship Passenger Manifests, 1820-1880,* 1983.

Gary J. Zimmerman and Marion Wolfert. *German Immigrants: Lists of Passengers Bound from Bremen to New York, 1847-1854,* 1985.

Printed departure records from Europe are also available. They range from works on the colonial period, such as John C. Hotten's *The Original Lists of Persons of Quality;...and Others Who Went From Great Britain to the American Plantations, 1600-1700....* (1874, reprinted 1974), which is taken from manuscripts in the British Public Record Office, to works covering the nineteenth century such as Robert P. Swierenga's *Dutch Emigrants to the United States, South Africa, South America, and Southeast Asia, 1835-1880* (1983), and *The Wuerttemberg Emigration Index* (1986+) by Trudy Schenk, and Ruth Froelke.

Three other books may assist researchers interested in immigration and passenger lists. Two are steamship directories: The *Morton Allen Directory* (1931) lists European passenger steamship arrivals 1890-1930, and *Adler's Directory* (1940) lists passenger steamships from Europe to Eastern U. S. ports, 1899-1929. The third book is Michael J. Anuta's *Ships of Our Ancestors* (1983), a volume of pictures and photographs of nineteenth and twentieth century passenger ships.

NATURALIZATION RECORDS

Only a small number of naturalization records have been transcribed and published; the vast majority remain in the courts or have been transferred to National Archives branches. The one major body of naturalization records which has appeared in print is *Philadelphia Naturalization Records* (1982) for the years 1789-1880. Anyone planning to use naturalization records should first consult two works: *Searching for Your Immigrant Ancestor: A Guide to Naturalization Records* (1975) by James C. and Lila L. Neagles, and the very important *American Naturalization Processes and Procedures 1790-1985* (1985) by John J. Newman. Newman explains the process of naturalization using many examples and illustrations. The work also includes an extremely useful bibliographical essay. More and more transcriptions of naturalization records are appearing in print, and the Newberry is actively collecting them. They can be located in the library's Card Catalogue in two ways: "[Name of location (city, county, or state)]--Genealogy," or "Naturalization Records--[Name of location]."

CHAPTER 9

SPECIAL NEWBERRY LIBRARY SOURCES

THE LOCAL AND FAMILY HISTORY SECTION

The Genealogical Index of The Newberry Library

The Genealogical Index of The Newberry Library, published by G. K. Hall and Company in 1960, is an extremely valuable research tool in local and family history. The four volumes of the *Genealogical Index* contain about 1 million entries for family names found in selected Newberry Library volumes. The *Genealogical Index* is not, however, a catalogue of the library's holdings. It was compiled between 1896 and 1918, and as a result does not contain references to any book published after 1918. Entries were originally written on slips of paper which were inserted into large binders which hung on the wall. The original "Wall Index," as it was commonly known, no longer exists.

The *Genealogical Index* is arranged in alphabetical order by surname, and each surname is broken down by regions, states, and allied families. References on families and individuals from genealogies, local histories, and periodicals are included, with some entries for Great Britain and Europe. The information found in a single entry varies from a biographical sketch in a county history to a several-page genealogy from a New England town history or merely a name on a muster roll or list of taxpayers. The entries are most useful as clue-finders for family history research, and the *Genealogical Index* does provide access to many books which lack indexes, including many county histories.

The *Genealogical Index* is available in many libraries, and because many of the cited books are found in other libraries, researchers need not rely solely on the Newberry collection to check entries. The entries do not give full author and title information and may appear somewhat cryptic, although with a little effort most can be deciphered. The call numbers which appear are those used by The Newberry Library only, although researchers are cautioned that many of the call numbers have been changed since 1918 and should be verified in the Card Catalogue.

The following examples, taken from the *Genealogical Index,* will show how to identify citations and the sort of information contained in entries.

Tuck Family
Charlestown, Mass. (Wyman, T. B.) 1879: *2*: 956   E6918.9

Researchers will *not* find this reference by looking under "Tuck Family" in the Card Catalogue. Looking under "Charlestown, Massachusetts" in the Card Catalogue, one will find *The Genealogies and Estates of Charlestown, in the County of Middlesex and Commonwealth of Massachusetts, 1629-1818* by Thomas Bellows Wyman, published in 1879. In this particular case, the call number has not been changed. Information on a Thomas Tuck, and his family, appears on page 956 of volume 2.

Tuck Family
Bowie Fam. (Bowie, W. W.) 1899: See Index E7.B68

To examine this entry, researchers should check the Card Catalogue under "Bowie Family," where they will find *The Bowies and Their Kindred* by Walter Worthington Bowie, published in 1899. A check of the book's index reveals a reference on page 388 to Margaret Sprigg Bowie Chew, who married Judge William Hallam Tuck in 1843.

Local and Family History Vertical File

One of the Local and Family History Section's lesser known holdings is its collection of material in the Vertical File. The Vertical File consists of pamphlets, manuscript genealogical papers, some family newsletters, and other miscellaneous items which the library wishes to keep, but cannot bind and catalogue. The quantity of material, on both surnames and geographical areas, in each file ranges from a few sheets to several archives boxes, and the quality and usability also varies.

Access is through the Vertical File card catalogue. This file is divided into two sections: "Family History" and "Local History." The catalogue cards provide little or no descriptive information, so items must be paged and examined to determine their contents. In addition, all material on a single surname is filed in the same folder, even though the items may refer to several unrelated families. Therefore, in a single folder, researchers may find a fifteen-page pamphlet genealogy, a transcription from a family Bible, and a biographical sketch pertaining to three different unrelated families who happen to share the same surname. Several large, unique collections of genealogical manuscript material are also found in the Vertical File. For a list of those collections see Chapter 2.

Heraldry File

The Newberry Library has a card index to pictures of coats-of-arms appearing in selected Newberry books. This file, which has about 75,000 entries, was compiled by Joseph C. Wolf, heraldic artist and long-time head of the Local and Family History Section. Most of the entries are for surnames, but some civic and ecclesiastical arms are also included. The largest number of entries is for English coats-of-arms, although other countries are also represented. The cards are arranged in alphabetical order and include the call number and page number of the book in which the picture appears. Pictures which are in color are noted. Some cards have additional information such as the country from which the coat-of-arms originates. Only a small percentage of the cards lists the title of the book in which the picture appears, and this can present some problems when a book's call number has been changed. No new entries have been added to the file since Joseph Wolf's retirement in 1974.

Unfortunately, there is no list of the books which Wolf consulted in compiling his file. A variety of works were searched including many of the peerages and baronetages, the English visitations and local histories (both British and American), some family genealogies, heraldic journals and other magazines including *Gentleman's Magazine* (London, 1731-1907), some of the English record society publications, the Harleian Society publications, most standard works on heraldry, but only a few of the armorials. One major armorial which is included is Alberto and Arturo Garcia-Caraffa's *Enciclopedia Heraldica y Genealogica Hispano-Americana,* 88 volumes (1919-63).

The Chicago and Cook County Biography and Industry File

In the early 1980s, the Local and Family History Section began compiling an index to biographical sketches appearing in selected Chicago and Cook County collective biographies. County histories, containing biographical sketches, were quite popular in rural areas in the late nineteenth century. Likewise, collective biographies were also published for citizens of urban areas. Although many of the works consist primarily of sketches of such prominent figures as George Pullman, Marshall Field, and Potter Palmer, others focus on ethnic, occupational, religious, political, and fraternal groups. The biographies of hundreds of everyday people are recorded, although the majority are middle or upper middle class. These latter works on everyday people have been the main focus of the Newberry indexing project.

Mentioning just a few of the books already indexed will give researchers some idea of the variety of published biographical sources that are available: *Chicago und Sein Deutschthum* (1902); *Memorials of Deceased Companions of the Commandery of the State of Illinois,* 3 volumes (1901-23), by the Military Order of the Loyal Legion; *History of Chicago and Souvenir of the Liquor Interest* (1891); *The Swedish Element in Illinois* (1917); and *History of Kehillath Anshe Maarabh* (1897). Books selected for the File were published prior to 1930 and are indexed in their entirety. That is, all subjects of biographies are included, regardless of their connection to Chicago or Cook County, with the exception of sketches of U. S. Presidents.

The File presently contains over 7,000 entries, mostly for individuals, and new entries are continually being added. The File is arranged alphabetically, and each entry contains birthdate, deathdate, and name of spouse, if given in the sketch, making it easier to differentiate people with the same name. Notation is also made when a portrait of the individual appears. The Chicago and Cook County Biography and Industry File has already proved useful to many genealogists, historians, librarians, and researchers seeking biographical information on nineteenth and early twentieth century Chicago area residents. Researchers are encouraged to check the File periodically as new entries are added.

THE DEPARTMENT OF SPECIAL COLLECTIONS

The Department of Special Collections at The Newberry Library houses several categories of material that may be of use to local and family history researchers. These include rare books, modern manuscripts, maps (covered in Chapter 2), the railroad archives, and certain separate collections such as the Ayer and Graff collections. Special Collections does not maintain a separate card catalogue, and all books housed in Special Collections can be located through the library's main card catalogues. Due to the unique or rare nature of the material, special rules govern its use.

Four areas of the Department of Special Collections are of particular interest: Modern Manuscripts, the Railroad Archives, the Edward E. Ayer collection, and the Everett D. Graff collection. The great western historian Ray Allen Billington said that the combination of the Graff and Ayer collections made the Newberry one of the two or three outstanding libraries for the study of the American West.

The Edward E. Ayer Collection

Edward E. Ayer was a member of the first board of trustees of The Newberry Library and the first donor of a great collection to the library. The major thrust of the collection is the relations between Europeans and native peoples in North and South America, the Caribbean Islands, Hawaii, and the Philippines. The collection was given to the Newberry in 1911 and consisted of approximately 17,000 pieces. It presently contains over 95,000 volumes and continues to grow.

The Newberry's great holdings of American Indian material are part of the Ayer collection. Local and family history researchers may find of interest works on early explorations, missionary efforts, travel and description accounts, Indian captivity narratives (see Chapter 10), plus many rare maps and manuscripts. The collection also contains histories, biographical dictionaries, and some genealogical material on Latin America. A *Dictionary Catalog of the Edward E. Ayer Collection of Americana and American Indians in The Newberry Library* has been published in sixteen volumes and two supplements (1961-80). It includes author and subject entries, with the exception of the East Indian, Philippine, Hawaiian, and Linguistics collections. Also available are checklists of Ayer maps and manuscripts.

The Everett D. Graff Collection

Everett D. Graff (1885-1964) was a book collector and former President of the Board of The Newberry Library. His collection of 10,000 books and manuscripts, many extremely rare, deals with the exploration and settlement of the frontier in nineteenth-century America. Additions are still being made to the Graff collection. Although the bulk of the collection deals with the trans-Mississippi West, there is some very important material on the Midwest, much of it quite rare. There is also an interesting collection of Alaska material. The collection is particularly rich for travel narratives, early town, county, and state histories, early directories, gold rush literature, material on the Mormons, the fur trade, mining, the cattle industry, law enforcement, early state imprints, and military activities. It also includes a strong collection on Iowa, reflecting Mr. Graff's interest in his native state.

Researchers may wish to refer to *A Catalogue of the Everett D. Graff Collection of Western Americana* (1968), compiled by Colton Storm. The catalogue does not include every item in the Graff collection, but entries appear for 4,801 items--source materials and secondary works of exceptional interest.

Modern Manuscripts

The Newberry Library's Modern Manuscript Collection consists of over 150 separate collections reflecting the literary, musical, and historical development of the Midwest. The collections cover various time periods from the eighteenth century to the mid-twentieth century and vary in size from a single item to huge quantities of material. The Modern Manuscript Collection reflects the library's printed book collection and concentrates on the personal papers of nineteenth and twentieth century individuals, most with Midwestern associations. Well represented are literary figures, musicians, newspaper people, and Chicago literary and social organizations. No papers of fraternal, benevolent, or ethnic organizations are held.

There are two means of accessing the collection. A set of binders labeled *Newberry Library Modern Manuscripts* is arranged by collection. The Modern Manuscripts card catalogue is arranged alphabetically by surname. It is highly recommended, however, that those wishing to use Modern Manuscripts material seek assistance from the Curator of Modern Manuscripts or the Special Collections staff. The Newberry does report its manuscript holdings to the *National Union Catalog of Manuscript Collections.*

Although at first glance it may appear that the Modern Manuscripts Collection has little of interest for local and family historians, there are in fact a number of collections which contain family correspondence, journals, diaries, and travel accounts. Although most of the families eventually had some midwestern association, there is a great deal of material on families and individuals in the East. A few of the collections with especially large or significant holdings of family material are listed below. Researchers should be aware that material by or about allied or associated families will frequently be found in the manuscript collections, in addition to items relating to the main subject of the collection. For more detailed information on a particular collection consult the set of *Newberry Library Modern Manuscript* binders or the Curator of Modern Manuscripts.

A Selected List of Modern Manuscript Collections

Edward Eagle Brown Family (includes a sea captain, Chicago   jurist, and banker, 1715-1959)

Thomas Butler Carter Letters (from Chicago to Newark, New Jersey, 1831-98)

Annie Cox to G. W. Allen Correspondence (Wisconsin and Michigan, 1862-65)

Ephraim C. Dawes (Civil War and Midwest, c. 1860s-1900)

Robert Everett Family (material on abolition, women's rights, temperance, 1820-1930)

Henry Flentye (Chicago and suburban land purchase documents, 1852-1915)

Rudolph Ganz (Swiss family of pioneer photographers, an art historian, and a musician, 1886-1972)

Frederick Gookin Family (Chicago family, *Mayflower* descendants, 1864-1922)

N. W. Harris Family (prominent banking family of Chicago/Lake Geneva, 1880-1970)

Carter H. Harrison IV (mayor of Chicago, also some family letters from Ohio, 1731-1953)

Milo Kendall (large, unprocessed nineteenth-century family collection)

Raven McDavid Papers (Includes field notes for the Linguistic Atlas of the north-central states, middle and south Atlantic states. Notes sometimes include genealogical information provided by interviewees.)

Capt. Christopher Gardner Pearce (Civil War letters)

Eugene Ernst Prussing (Chicago lawyer and author, 1855-1927)

Hermann Raster and Wilhelm Rapp (editors of the *Illinois Staats-Zeitung*)

Charles and Albina Rich letters (Rich family of Milo, Maine, 1853-54)

Rodgers Family (several seafarers and pioneers, 1773-1925)

Platt Rogers Spencer (Ohio, 1836-1953)

Waller Family (Kentucky and Chicago, 1803-87)

Chauncey Whittelsey (Connecticut commercial records, 1707-1852)

Woods Family (Loyalists, Boone County, Illinois pioneers, Gold Rush letters, 1780-1973)

Railroad Archives

The Department of Special Collections holds the archives of the Chicago, Burlington and Quincy Railroad, the Illinois Central Railroad, and the Pullman Company. Although much of the material consists of central office records and correspondence which will have little interest for local and family history researchers, some archival material may be of potential value. In addition to the printed guides listed below, the staff of the Department of Special Collections should be consulted by those interested in further information on these archival records.

Chicago, Burlington and Quincy

Of the two railroad collections, the Burlington archives has more material of interest to local and family history researchers. A good place to begin is with the *Guide to the Burlington Archives in The Newberry*

Library, 1851-1901 (1949), compiled by Elisabeth Coleman Jackson and Carolyn Curtis. The collection consists of central office and land office records, including letters, ledgers, account books, and operating books. There is little on railroad employees, with the exception of payrolls for all divisions from 1889-1900. Some information on towns along the Burlington route can also be found. An example is letters "from Osceola [Iowa] citizens about stone quarries, October 24, 1885-June 10, 1886" (*Guide*, p. 61).

Of most interest is the material on the activities of land companies, mostly in Nebraska and Iowa, and to a lesser degree in Missouri. These private real estate companies handled land sales for the private investment of railroad officials and friends, both before and after construction of the road. Twenty-five private land companies are included. The largest amount of material is on the Iowa Land Association and the South Platte Land Company. Records consist of land and town lot books, contracts and sales records and letters from agents.

Also available is material on the Burlington and Missouri River Railroad Company, Land Department. The Burlington was granted about 390,000 acres in Iowa in 1856, plus over two million more acres in Nebraska in 1864. Included in the records of the Land Department are applications to buy land, descriptions of land, sales and purchaser records, pre-emption cases, disputed claims, and letters to prospective settlers.

The Burlington also cooperated with steamship companies and had agents and offices in Europe to encourage farmers to emigrate to the Midwest. Sample land circulares, letters to individuals and groups thinking of emigrating, and letters to agents can all be found in the collection.

Illinois Central

Research into the Illinois Central archives should begin with *Guide to the Illinois Central Archives in The Newberry Library, 1851-1906* (1951), compiled by Carolyn Curtis Mohr. The Illinois Central material consists of central office papers, land company records (not as useful as the Burlington land office records), records of subsidiary rail lines and other companies (including several coal, mining, and construction companies), plus very limited personnel material.

The personnel material consists of some early payroll vouchers and some early letters of application from engineers. The records of the Illinois Central Land Department include lists of lands sold and conveyed, records of sales, and letters from purchasers and agents for land in Illinois, Iowa, Mississippi, Kentucky, and Louisiana. Private land company records exist for the Iowa Homestead Company, Iowa Land and Loan Company, Iowa Railroad Land Company, and Southern Land and Investment Company (Iowa). Records include contracts, land sales, and mortgages.

Pullman Company

Presently there is no published guide to the archives of the Pullman Company. Three categories of material are included in the archives: records of service employees, including porters; yard records, which include car cleaners; and repair shop records--the largest body of material in the collection. The collection consists primarily of payroll records and employment records for six Pullman repair shops.

The repair shops are:

1. Calumet (Chicago), 1901-67. Pre-World War I employment records appear to be about fifty percent complete, while post-World War II records appear to be about ninety percent complete.

2. Wilmington, Delaware, 1900-58.

3. St. Louis, 1900-66.

4. Richmond, California, 1911-58. All employment records for surnames A-E are missing.

5. Atlanta, cannot be located at present time.

6. Buffalo, New York, 1900-58. Employment records are not in alphabetical order at present time.

The information found in these employment records varies greatly, both among the different shops and over time. The Calumet and St. Louis shop records have an employment packet for each employee, which is generally more informative than records from other shops which have only the employee service card. A *good* record *might* contain country of birth, date of birth, date of marriage, employment history, medical records, picture of the employee, and insurance beneficiaries. Employment records are also available for many service and yard employees, including car cleaners, porters, and district employees.

CHAPTER 10

MISCELLANEOUS COLLECTIONS AT THE NEWBERRY LIBRARY

THE LYMAN C. DRAPER MANUSCRIPTS

The Newberry Library has on microfilm the Lyman C. Draper Manuscripts from the State Historical Society of Wisconsin. The Draper Manuscripts deal with the trans-Allegheny West from the mid-1700s to the War of 1812 and consist of nearly 500 volumes of records divided into fifty series. Only about one quarter of the material is original records--diaries and journals, maps, surveyors' notes, military documents, muster rolls, and personal papers of families and individuals. The bulk of the collection is material "noted, copied or generated by Draper during his own research, mainly from 1840 to 1891,"[1] and consists of notes, letters, interviews, reminiscences, and transcriptions of documents.

The Draper Manuscripts are a major source of information on the pioneer period in the trans-Allegheny West, but have not been fully exploited by historians or genealogists. One work which does make good use of the Draper Manuscripts is Ella Hazel Spraker's *The Boone Family...* (1922, reprinted 1974). Because the Draper is a manuscript collection, there is no single, all-inclusive index to every name, place, and event mentioned. Thus, researchers must be prepared to spend some time working through the material. Fortunately, there is now a very ex-

cellent, detailed *Guide to the Draper Manuscripts* (1983) by Josephine L. Harper. Anyone wishing to use the Draper Manuscripts must consult this volume. In addition, the State Historical Society of Wisconsin has published printed calendars for five of the series:
Calendar of the Tennessee and King's Mountain Papers of the Draper Collection of Manuscripts (1929).

Mabel C. Weaks, comp. *Calendar of the Kentucky Papers of the Draper Collection of Manuscripts (1925).*

_____. *The Preston and Virginia Papers of the Draper Collection of Manuscripts* (1915).

NOTES
1. Josephine L. Harper, *Guide to the Draper Manuscripts* (Madison: State Historical Society of Wisconsin, 1983), p. xvi.

INDIAN CAPTIVITY NARRATIVES

Accounts of individuals taken captive by North American Indians have existed since the late seventeenth century. Although there is only a remote possibility that one's ancestor or subject of research was taken captive and left a record of his or her experience, these very fascinating narratives provide yet one more possible source of information for the local and family historian. To gain some perspective on the number of captives taken, researchers may wish to refer to a study by Alden T. Vaughan and Daniel K. Richter which determined that 1,641 New Englanders were captured between 1675 and 1763, although it must be kept in mind that not all recorded their experience.[2]

The Newberry Library is the best place in the country to study these works. Indian captivity narratives were very popular; several were even best sellers, in part because of their exotic settings and tales of adventure. The experiences of more than 500 captives have been recorded, from colonial New England to the nineteenth century Southwest. Nearly all of these recorded narratives are available at the Newberry, beginning with the earliest, Mrs. Mary Rowlandson's *The Soveraignty and Goodness of God, Together with the Faithfulness of His Promises Displayed: Being a Narrative of the Captivity and Restauration of Mrs. Mary Rowlandson...,* published in 1682.

The best introductions to the captivity narratives are Robert W. G. Vail's *The Voice of the Old Frontier* (1949) and Alden T. Vaughan's *Narratives of North American Indian Captivity: A Selective Bibliography* (1983), which is also a guide to descriptive and analytical literature. The library's collection of secondary materials on Indian captivity narratives is outstanding.

These narratives are located in the Card Catalogue under the subject heading "Indians of North America--Captivities" or under "[Tribal

Name]--Captivities" (e.g., "Miami Indians--Captivities," "Cherokee Indians--Captivities"). About eighty-five percent of the captivity narratives are in the Edward E. Ayer Collection, while the remaining ones are in the Everett D. Graff and General collections. The Newberry also has the Garland Library of Narratives of North American Indian Captivities, which reproduces 311 titles, nearly all of which are also found at the library in their original editions. Captivity narratives can also be found within sets and collections. A number appear, for example, in the *Pennsylvania Archives* and *Michigan Pioneer and Historical Collections*.

NOTES
2. Alden T. Vaughan and Daniel K. Richter, "Crossing the Cultural Divide: Indians and New Englanders, 1605-1763," *Proceedings of the American Antiquarian Society* 90 (1980): 23-99.

SOURCE MATERIAL FROM THE GENEALOGICAL DEPARTMENT OF THE CHURCH OF JESUS CHRIST OF LATTER-DAY SAINTS

The genealogical activities of the Church of Jesus Christ of Latter-day Saints (Mormons or LDS) and their massive library in Salt Lake City are well known to genealogical researchers and many historians. Several items generated by, or written about the LDS Library and the Genealogical Department are part of The Newberry Library collection. These materials can be identified in the Card Catalogue under several different headings, reflecting name changes that have occurred: "Genealogical Society of the Church of Jesus Christ of Latter-day Saints," "Genealogical Society of Utah," and "Church of Jesus Christ of Latter-day Saints--Genealogical Department."

The Newberry has two very significant items from the LDS. The first is the International Genealogical Index (IGI), an index to names found in computerized files of the Genealogical Department. This microfiche set, which is periodically updated, includes over 88 million names from over ninety countries. Entries are taken from government records, including records of birth and marriage, selected records submitted by LDS members, parish records, some LDS Temple Records, and other miscellaneous sources.

The second important item is the Genealogical Library Catalog (GLC), which is a catalog and guide to the holdings of the LDS Genealogical Library in Salt Lake City. The GLC includes both printed works and records microfilmed by the LDS throughout the world. The GLC is on microfiche, is periodically updated, and supersedes the Newberry's copy of the *Microfilmed Catalog: United States and*

Canadian Collection, 1973 edition. The GLC is divided into four parts: surname catalog, author/title catalog, locality catalog, and subject catalog. Primary emphasis has been placed on the locality catalog. One interesting feature of the locality catalog is the list of place names appearing at the beginning of each country or state. This list may prove helpful in determining the location of a town, particularly in foreign countries. The GLC lets researchers determine what records have been microfilmed by the LDS and are, therefore, available through their branch library system.

A number of handbooks for genealogical research and guides to the LDS Library are also part of the Newberry collection. Extremely useful is the published series of finding aids to the microfilmed manuscript collections of the Genealogical Society of Utah. This series, still in progress, has already produced descriptive inventories or surveys of the Mexican, German, English, New York, French, Mexican colonial parish registers, Guatemalan, and New Hampshire collections.

Several other items also deserve mention. The library has a few miscellaneous compilations of genealogical records, mostly marriages and cemetery transcriptions, done by the Genealogical Society of Utah. Also available is *The Utah Genealogical and Historical Magazine,* 31 volumes (1910-40), published by the Genealogical Society of Utah. In 1980 the LDS sponsored a World Conference on Records, entitled "Preserving our Heritage." Speakers from throughout the world presented papers on a variety of subjects. Most, but not all, of these conference papers were reproduced in a thirteen-volume set and provide an excellent resource on new trends, sources, and thinking in family history.

MAIL ORDER CATALOGUES

Mail order catalogues are a seldom-used, but potentially useful and interesting source for historians in many fields, as well as genealogists. Such catalogues began as a method for selling to rural customers and can provide valuable information on social life and customs, fashion, and prices. They may help identify farm implements, household goods, furniture, sporting goods, and clothing.

The Newberry has catalogues from two major mail order firms: Sears, Roebuck and Company, and Montgomery Ward and Company. Sears, Roebuck and Company catalogues are available on microfilm from 1892 to the present. They began as watch and jewelry catalogues, and later added other lines of merchandise. The library has three different catalogues from the Chicago-based Montgomery Ward and Company. General catalogues from 1872-1985, the Christmas catalogues from 1934-85, and specialty catalogues from 1886-1985 are all available on microfilm.

CHAPTER 11

NEW ENGLAND

From its earliest days, The Newberry Library has had an interest in, and collected works on New England. Many important figures in the early history of the library, including the first Librarian, William Frederick Poole, had New England origins and interests, and Walter Loomis Newberry, after whom the Library is named, was born in Connecticut. Nearly one hundred years of collecting works on New England has made the Newberry one of the country's leading libraries for the study of New England local history and genealogy.

The Newberry's New England holdings are strongest for the Colonial, Revolutionary, and early Federal periods. A great deal is available on religion, church history, description and travel accounts, Indian captivity narratives, published diaries, letters and personal narratives, and military affairs. The collection of historical periodicals is also quite strong, both for local history periodicals, and state and regional journals. This includes, of course, the *New England Historic Genealogical Register* (1847+) and many of the Genealogical Publishing Company anthologies taken from its pages. The Newberry researcher can expect to find all significant historical works, many works of lesser importance, numerous rare and unusual items, and nearly all collective genealogical works on New England.

Of great importance to New England researchers has been the outstanding work of the Committee for a New England Bibliography. The Committee has sponsored publication of historical bibliographies for Maine, Massachusetts, New Hampshire, Rhode Island, and Vermont. A volume on Connecticut and an area volume on New England will appear in the future. These works provide an excellent starting point for researchers who will find a great many of the cited works at the Newberry. Other research guides and bibliographies for particular states are covered in the chapters on each state. The family history researcher will find several area guides available. Four of the more useful are: Norman Wright's *Genealogy in America*, volume I (1968) which covers Massachusetts, Connecticut, and Maine; *Genealogical Research: Methods and Sources*, 2 volumes, revised (1980-83), by the American Society of Genealogists; the *Genealogists' Handbook for New England Research*, 2nd edition (1985), a handy location guide to sources; and *Genealogical Research in New England*, edited by Ralph J. Crandall (1984).

In recent years New England has been a popular subject for community and demographic studies, and the Newberry has very actively collected such works. A very fine guide to these recent studies is Ronald D. Kerr's "New England Community Studies Since 1960: A Bibliography," *New England Historic Genealogical Register*, 138 (July and October 1984). The Newberry has few of the dissertations listed, but nearly everything else.

Two major compilations that cover all of New England are of particular importance to family history researchers, but are also useful to biographers and local historians. *The Greenlaw Index of the New England Historic Genealogical Society* (1979) is a first and last name index to over one thousand volumes of New England genealogy and local history, most of which can be consulted at the Newberry. The second compilation is Clarence A. Torrey's *New England Marriages Prior to 1700*. The Newberry has both the microfilm and the 1985 printed version. While the printed version is easier to read, the microfilm copy does cite the sources of the marriage information. Torrey's work contains over 35,000 names and is believed to include almost all seventeenth century New England marriages found in printed sources.

Also of value to researchers are the genealogical queries columns that have appeared in the *Boston Evening Transcript* and the *Hartford Times*. The column in the *Transcript* appeared between 1896 and 1941, while the *Hartford Times* column appeared between 1934 and 1967.

CONNECTICUT

Connecticut researchers are fortunate to have available an extensive amount of published material on the local and family history of that state. Gary Boyd Roberts, of the New England Historic Genealogical Society, has called Connecticut records the "best organized, most completely documented, with largest corpus of definitive published works."[1]

Several large, important collections, both in book form and on microfilm, are available at the Newberry. The best known is the "Lucius B. Barbour Collection of Connecticut Vital Records before 1850." This microfilm set has two sections; one is arranged by town, and the other is a state-wide alphabetical surname list. This collection includes all Connecticut towns, except for a few, such as New Haven, whose vital records have been published separately. The Charles R. Hale collection, on 358 reels of microfilm, consists of obituaries and marriage notices from Connecticut newspapers and tombstone inscriptions from over 2,000 cemeteries. Most of the citations deal with events up to the Civil War period. Important published collections include *The Public Records of the Colony of Connecticut,* 15 volumes (1850-90); *The Public Records of the State of Connecticut,* 10 volumes (1894-1965); and *Collections of the Connecticut Historical Society,* 31 volumes (1860-1967).

Genealogical works began to appear very early in Connecticut and include Royal Hinman's *Catalogue of the Names of the First Puritan Settlers of the Colony of Connecticut* (1846) and Nathaniel Goodwin's *Genealogical Notes...of Some of the First Settlers of Connecticut* (1856). This interest in genealogy was continued in the twentieth century by Donald Lines Jacobus, one of America's foremost genealogists. Jacobus produced many important works including *Families of Ancient New Haven* (1922-32, reprinted 1974), which was continued as the journal *The American Genealogist.* Another useful source for Connecticut researchers is the genealogical queries column which appeared in the *Hartford Times.* This column is available at the Newberry for the years 1934-67.

The Newberry's holdings of Connecticut state and local histories are extensive and very strong. Many early state histories are available such as *A General History of Connecticut* (1781) by Samuel A. Peters, and Benjamin Trumbull's *A Complete History of Connecticut* (1797), a fine narrative account of the period. Most Connecticut towns have published histories which can be found at the library. Numerous publications of the Connecticut Historical Society are available, as well as many recent monographs produced by scholars and academic historians on various aspects of Connecticut local and family history. Another source is the pamphlet series produced by the Connecticut Tercentenary Commission, Committee on Historical Publications. Also available is the Connecticut Bicentennial Series, which consists of thirty-five volumes on various aspects of Connecticut's involvement in the Revolution.

In addition to printed histories, researchers will find directories, historical addresses, publications of local historical societies, extensive works on church history, and printed editions of the papers of important Connecticut figures. A transcript on microfilm of the Stamford Town Meeting Records from 1640-1806 is also available. *The Connecticut Register,* also called *Green's Annual Register,* lists militia officers, justices of the peace, clergy and judges, and provides other information on local and state government officials and activities. The Newberry has thirty-eight scattered volumes from 1800 to 1857 and complete holdings from 1887-1971. One other source will be of interest not only to Connecticut researchers, but also to those interested in Pennsylvania. *The*

Susquehanna Company Papers, edited by Julian P. Boyd and Robert J. Taylor, 11 volumes (1930-71), deals with a disputed part of northeastern Pennsylvania, settled mostly from Connecticut in the last half of the eighteenth century.

Bibliographies and Guides

Elizabeth Abbe. "Connecticut Genealogical Research: Sources and Suggestions." *New England Historic Genealogical Register* 134 (January 1980): 3-26. Contains a selected list of printed Connecticut vital records. Reprinted in *Genealogical Research in New England,* Ralph J. Crandall, ed., 1984.

Thomas Kemp. *Connecticut Researcher's Handbook,* 1981.

Kip Sperry. *Connecticut Sources for Family Historians,* 1980.

Periodical and Serial Publications

Connecticut Ancestry (formerly *Stamford Genealogical Society Bulletin*), 1961 (vol. 3) to date.

The Connecticut Magazine, 1895-1908. A magazine "devoted to Connecticut in its various phases of history, literature, scenic beauty, art, science, industry."

The Connecticut Nutmegger (Connecticut Society of Genealogists), 1968 to date.

Papers of the New Haven Colony Historical Society. 10 vols., 1865-1951.

New Haven Historical Society Journal, 1967 (vol. 16) to date.

NOTES
1. Gary Boyd Roberts, "Some Reflections on Modern Connecticut Genealogical Scholarship," *The Connecticut Nutmegger* 12 (December 1979): 371.

MAINE

Maine was part of the state of Massachusetts until 1820; therefore, some information on early Maine will be found in works on Massachusetts.

Many important documents of Maine's early history have been transcribed and published and can be consulted at The Newberry Library. *Documentary History of the State of Maine* (1869-1916) is a twenty-four volume set comprised of information taken from the Massachusetts Archives. *Province and Court Records of Maine,* 6 volumes (1928-64), covers early Maine court records from 1636-1727. *Maine Wills* (1887) by William M. Sargent covers the period 1640-1760, and *The Probate Records of Lincoln County, Maine* (1895), edited by William

David Patterson, covers 1760-1800. York County deeds for the years 1642-1737 have also been published in the eighteen-volume set, *York Deeds* (1903-10).

An important resource for local and family historians and biographers is the cemetery transcriptions produced by the Maine Old Cemetery Association. To date two series (ten microfilm reels) have been published. These transcripts cover several thousand mostly small cemeteries throughout the state. For more information on early settlers see Charles Pope's *The Pioneers of Maine and New Hampshire* (1908), and *Genealogical Dictionary of Maine and New Hampshire* (1928-39) by Sybil Noyes, Charles Thornton Libby, and Walter Goodwin Davis.

The Newberry has extensive holdings of Maine state and town histories, including the first history of Maine, James Sullivan's *The History of the District of Maine* (1795). Local histories range over time from William White's *History of Belfast, Maine* (1827), to the great outpouring of town histories occasioned by the Bicentennial. Few county histories have been published, but most of them will be found at the library. Published vital records are available for only about two dozen Maine towns, and the Newberry has all of them except for the towns of Augusta, Bowdoin, and Winslow. The library's holdings also include a great deal of description and travel literature from the earliest period through the nineteenth century and much material on the separation of Maine from Massachusetts and the Constitutional Convention.

One final source that deserves mention is Harry Edward Mitchell's *Town Registers*. These registers, published between 1900 and 1911, are partly histories, partly directories, and partly lists of organizations. Of the 179 towns covered by Mitchell, the Newberry has the registers for seventy-two.

Bibliographies and Guides

Committee for a New England Bibliography. *Maine: A Bibliography of its History,* 1977. Excellent.

John E. Frost. *Maine Genealogy,* 1977. Very good.

_____. "Maine Genealogy: Some Distinctive Aspects." *New England Historic Genealogical Register* 131 (October 1977): 243-66. Very good. Includes a checklist of some Maine genealogies. Reprinted in *Genealogical Research in New England,* Ralph J. Crandall, ed., 1984.

Maine History Bibliographical Guide Series. Six volumes on topics such as Indians, shipbuilding, the colonial period, and the Civil War.

Edward Schriver. "Maine: A Bibliographic Review." *Acadiensis* 5 (Spring 1976): 154-62.

Joseph Williamson. *A Bibliography of the State of Maine from the Ear-*

liest Period to 1891, 1896.

Periodical and Serial Publications

Acadiensis, 1971 to date. "Journal of the history of the Atlantic Region," published by the University of New Brunswick.

Publications of the Gorges Society of Portland. 5 vols., 1884-93.

Maine Genealogist and Biographer, 1875-78.

Maine Historical and Genealogical Recorder, 1884-98.

Maine Historical Magazine (formerly *Bangor Historical Magazine*), 1885-95.

Maine Historical Society Collections. 22 vols., 1831-1906. Includes articles on Maine history, biography, politics, and genealogy.

Maine Historical Society Quarterly, 1961 to date.

Sprague's Journal of Maine History, 1913-26.

MASSACHUSETTS

It was once written that the fabric of life in Massachusetts is woven with history. The amount of literature on the state is enormous, and not surprisingly, the Newberry's Massachusetts collection is the largest among the New England states. Much of the existing historical material is of high quality, beginning with the first contacts between Europeans and Indians, and extending through the nineteenth century.

Numerous historical organizations in the state have contributed to the mass of material on local and family history. One of the earliest and most prolific is the Massachusetts Historical Society which has been publishing works on Massachusetts for nearly two hundred years. The *Proceedings of the Massachusetts Historical Society,* (1791+); *Collections of the Massachusetts Historical Society,* (1792+); plus over fifty special publications of the Society are available at the Newberry. The Society has been particularly active in publishing the diaries, papers, letters, and correspondence of important figures in Massachusetts history. Other series published by historical organizations include the *Publications of the Colonial Society of Massachusetts* (1892+), which currently number over sixty volumes, and thirty-five volumes published by the Prince Society of Boston (1865-1911).

Historical writings on eastern Massachusetts are much more extensive than those for western Massachusetts. Thus an important source on the western and central parts of the state is the "Corbin Manuscript Collection in the New England Historic Genealogical Society," which is available on sixty reels of microfilm at the Newberry. This collection covers seventy-five villages and towns in western and central Massachusetts from the period 1650-1850.

Early town records and vital records are available for many locales. The Newberry has on microfilm copies of the original town records, to 1830, for Acton, Bedford, Carlisle, Concord, Gloucester, Lexington, and Lincoln. They include town meeting records, town order books, tax lists, assessors' records, treasurer's records, deeds, and selectmen's records. Published vital records to 1850 are available for over fifty percent of the older Massachusetts towns. Many of these were published early in this century by organizations such as the New England Historic Genealogical Society, The Essex Institute, and the Topsfield Historical Society. In recent years several organizations and individuals have published additional volumes. More towns are now available through a new series published by Jay M. Holbrook. The Holbrook series consists of microfiche copies of the original vital records to 1850. The Newberry has acquired dozens of towns in this series, including the extant Boston records for the years 1630-1849.

The Newberry Library collection is very strong in early accounts of Massachusetts, both in first and subsequent editions and printings, including such standards as *Good Newes from New England* (1624) by Edward Winslow and *Mourt's Relation* (1622). In recent years social, economic, and family historians have shown a great deal of interest in Massachusetts, particularly in the colonial period, and the Newberry has been quite active in collecting their works. A very fine guide to these recent studies is found in Ronald D. Kerr's "New England Community Studies Since 1960: A Bibliography," *New England Historic Genealogical Register,* 138 (July and October 1984). The Newberry has nearly everything Kerr cites, except for the dissertations.

There is a tremendous amount of material available on the Pilgrims. The General Society of Mayflower Descendants has published much of importance including *The Mayflower Quarterly* (1935+) and the very significant series in progress *Mayflower Families Through Five Generations* (1975+). *The Mayflower Descendant,* published by the Massachusetts Society of Mayflower Descendants, appeared in thirty-four volumes between 1899 and 1937. It resumed publication with volume 35 in 1985. One other useful source is *Genealogies of Mayflower Families,* 3 volumes (1985), selected by Gary Boyd Roberts. This work reproduces over 250 articles which have appeared in the *New England Historic Genealogical Register.* In addition, individual family genealogies exist on the Pilgrim families of Bradford, Brewster, Fuller, Hopkins and Howland. For more information on the Pilgrims and the Mayflower Society, see Chapter 7.

Some other useful sources are *The Massachusetts Magazine,* 1908-18, a magazine "devoted to Massachusetts history, genealogical biography"; *Massachusetts Tax Valuation List of 1771* (1978); and the genealogical queries column from the *Boston Evening Transcript* for the years 1896-1941. This column is indexed in the *American Genealogical-Biographical Index* (1952+). Published histories exist for most Massachusetts towns, and the Newberry's collection is outstanding. There are histories for all the Massachusetts counties, including a copy of one of the first county histories published in the United States, Peter Whitney's, *The History of the County of Worcester* (1793). Many important serial and periodical publications on Massachusetts local history can be found at the Newberry. These include well known works such as the *Report of the Record Commissioners of Boston,* 39 volumes (1876-1909), *Historical Collections of the Essex Institute* (1859+), and *Library of Cape Cod History and Genealogy,* 105 numbers (1909-30). Runs of the local historical society journal are available for Cambridge, Danvers, Dedham, Ipswich, Lynn, Medford, Nantucket, Pocumtuck Valley, Topsfield, and Worcester.

Bibliographies and Guides

Committee for a New England Bibliography. *Massachusetts: A Bibliography of its History,* 1976. Excellent.

Edward W. Hanson and Homer V. Rutherford. "Genealogical Research in Massachusetts: A Survey and Bibliographical Guide." *New England Historic Genealogical Register* 135 (July 1981): 163-98. Contains a bibliography of published and unpublished Massachusetts vital records. Reprinted in *Genealogical Research in New England,* Ralph J. Crandall, ed., 1984.

Published Official Records on Massachusetts

The Acts and Resolves, Public and Private, of the Province of the Massachusetts Bay. 21 vols., 1869-1922. Covers the years 1692-1780.

Journals of the House of Representatives of Massachusetts, 1919+. Over 50 volumes to date; coverage begins with the year 1715.

Plymouth Court Records, 1686-1859. 16 vols., 1978-81. Records for Plymouth County.

Records of the Colony of New Plymouth in New England. 12 vols., 1855-61. Covers the years 1620-92.

Records of the Court of Assistants of the Colony of the Massachusetts Bay. 3 vols., 1901-28. Covers the years 1630-92.

Records of the Governor and Company of the Massachusetts Bay. 5 vols., 1853-54. Covers the years 1628-86.

NEW HAMPSHIRE

The history of New Hampshire, its towns and people, has been covered quite well in published sources, a fine collection of which can be found at The Newberry Library. The colonial and early statehood periods are especially well covered in the Newberry holdings. Many early settlers of New Hampshire can be located in Charles H. Pope's *The Pioneers of Maine and New Hampshire* (1908) and in the *Genealogical Dictionary of Maine and New Hampshire* (1928-39) by Sybil Noyes, Charles Thornton Libby, and Walter Goodwin Davis. Several publications by Jay Holbrook list residents of eighteenth-century New Hampshire, and the *New Hampshire State and Provincial Papers,* 40 volumes (1867-1943), include New Hampshire probate records from 1635 to 1771, as well as many town and military records from the colonial period. A new source of information on New Hampshire residents is Glenn C. Towle's *New Hampshire Genealogical Digest, 1623-1900* (1986+), which contains abstracted biographies taken from works on New Hampshire. The fifteen volumes of the *Collections of the New Hampshire Historical Society* (1824-1939), are also part of the Newberry collection. Another interesting work, containing a variety of primary documents, biography, and history is John Farmer's and Jacob B. Moore's *Collections, Topographical, Historical and Biographical, Relating Principally to New-Hampshire,* 3 volumes (1822-24).

The Newberry has a very good collection of printed local histories. Histories for most southern New Hampshire towns can be found at the library. Fewer town histories have been published for the sparsely populated northern part of the state. Although few towns have published their vital records separately, a large number of the town histories do contain genealogical and vital records information. In addition to local histories, the researcher will also find some publications of local historical societies, among them the twelve volumes of *Manchester, New Hampshire Historic Association Collections* (1896-1910).

Another interesting local history resource is the *New Hampshire Register, Year Book, Almanac and Business Directory,* which, in addition to standard almanac information, includes lists of local government officials, churches, institutions, and other organizations throughout the state. The Newberry has copies of the *New Hampshire Register* for 1768, 1772, 1787-89, 1794-98, and 1800-1910.

Bibliographies and Guides

Allen H. Bent. *A Bibliography of The White Mountains,* 1911. Contains many references to *Appalachia,* the journal of the Appalachian Mountain Club, Boston. The Newberry has *Appalachia* for the years 1876-1917 (some issues lacking).

Committee for a New England Bibliography. *New Hampshire, A Bibliography of Its History,* 1979. Excellent. Supersedes Otis Hammond's *Check List of New Hampshire History* (1925).

David C. Dearborn. "New Hampshire Genealogy: A Perspective." *New England Historic Genealogical Register* 130 (October 1976): 244-58. Very helpful for both genealogists and historians.

Reprinted in *Genealogical Research in New England,* Ralph J. Crandall, ed., 1984.

Laird C. Towle. *New Hampshire Genealogical Research Guide,* 1983.

Periodical and Serial Publications

Granite Monthly. 62 vols., 1877-1930. "A magazine of history, biography, literature and state progress."

Historical New Hampshire, 1944 to date.

New Hampshire Genealogical Record, 1903-10. Short-lived, but of high quality.

RHODE ISLAND

Rhode Island, although the smallest of the states in geographical area, has generated a large quantity of writings on its local and family history. A number of series and multi-volume compilations of records and sources have been published, and all of them will be found at the Newberry. One of the best known is James N. Arnold's *Vital Records of Rhode Island, 1636-1850,* 21 volumes (1891-1912). This series is being continued by Alden G. Beaman's *Rhode Island Vital Records, New Series* (1975+). Another early work is *Rhode Island Historical Tracts,* 25 volumes in two series (1877-97), published by S. S. Rider.

Historical organizations have published several series that will be of value to researchers. Foremost among these is the Rhode Island Historical Society which has produced *Rhode Island Historical Society Collections,* 34 volumes (1827-1941); the quarterly journal *Rhode Island History* (1942+); and *Publications of the Rhode Island Historical Society,* 8 volumes (1893-1900). Other publications which can be found at The Newberry Library include *Papers From the Historical Seminary of Brown University,* 10 numbers (1894-99); the publications series of the Society of Colonial Wars, Rhode Island, which began in 1906 and now numbers over fifty titles; *Personal Narratives of Events in the War of the Rebellion,* published by the Rhode Island Soldiers and Sailors Historical Society in seven series (1878-1905); and *Publications of the Narragansett Club,* 6 volumes (1866-74), which reprinted the early writings of Rhode Islanders.

Several other items in the Newberry collection also deserve mention. For information on Rhode Island settlers before 1690, an essential work is John O. Austin's *Genealogical Dictionary of Rhode Island* (1887, reprinted with additions and corrections, 1969). Genealogists will also find *Genealogies of Rhode Island Families: From Rhode Island Periodicals* (1983) useful. This work reproduces articles from selected Rhode Island periodicals, all of which can be found at the Newberry. A small amount of material in the "Corbin Manuscript Collection" deals with

Rhode Island. For more information on this collection see the Massachusetts section of this guide. The library has a lengthy run of the *Manual with Rules and Orders for the Use of the General Assembly of the State of Rhode Island.* The Newberry's holdings cover 1867/68-1927/28, 1931-32. These manuals include lists of state officials, information on private societies, lists of judges, fees for liquor licenses, lists of lighthouses, plus much more.

The Newberry's holdings of local histories are quite good. In addition to secondary histories, researchers will also find the early records of several Rhode Island towns in print, including the four original towns, Providence, Warwick, Portsmouth and, Newport. Some of the compilations of Providence records are listed below.

Bibliographies and Guides

Committee for a New England Bibliography. *Rhode Island: A Bibliography of its History,* 1983. Has a very fine essay, "An Appraisal of Rhode Island Historiography."

Jane Fletcher Fiske. "Genealogical Research in Rhode Island." *New England Historic Genealogical Register* 136 (1982): 173-219. Very detailed; will be of use to local historians as well as genealogists. Reprinted in *Genealogical Research in New England,* Ralph J. Crandall, ed., 1984.

Kip Sperry. *Rhode Island Sources for Family Historians and Genealogists,* 1986.

Periodical and Serial Publications

The Narragansett Historical Register, 1882-91.

Bulletin of the Newport Historical Society, 1912-48.

Rhode Island Genealogical Register, 1978 to date.

Rhode Island Historical Magazine (formerly *The Newport Historical Magazine*), 1880-87.
Rhode Island History, 1942 to date.
Rhode Island Jewish Historical Notes, 1954 to date.

Providence and Providence Plantation Records

Alphabetical Index of the Births, Marriages and Deaths Recorded in Providence, 1636-1935. 35 vols., 1879-1940.

Early Records of the Town of Providence, 1636-1750. 21 vols., 1892-1915.

Records of the Colony of Rhode Island and Providence Plantations. 10 vols., 1856-65.

The library also has many eighteenth-century acts and resolves of

Rhode Island and Providence Plantation, both in original editions and facsimile.

VERMONT

Vermont, which became the fourteenth state in 1791, was the subject of much dispute between New Hampshire and New York, both of which tried to gain possession of the territory. For this reason, much relevant early Vermont material will be found in sources on those two states. One example is *The New Hampshire Grants, Being Transcripts of the Charters of Townships and Minor Grants of Lands Made By the Provincial Government of New Hampshire, Within the Present Boundaries of the State of Vermont, From 1749 to 1764*, which is volume 26 of the *New Hampshire State and Provincial Papers* (1895).

The Newberry has very good holdings on Vermont, including all the official published compendia dealing with the history of the state--the *State Papers of Vermont* (1918+), which includes land grants, petitions, and proceedings of the General Assembly; and the very important eight volumes of the *Records of the Governor and Council of the State of Vermont, 1775-1836* (1873-80), which contains much important pre-statehood and early statehood material.

The first published history of Vermont was *The Natural and Civil History of Vermont* (1794) by Samuel Williams. This volume is held by the library along with all other important state histories, among them another early work, Ira Allen's (Ethan's brother) *Natural and Political History of the State of Vermont* (1798). Many publications of the Vermont Historical Society are available, including a complete run of *Vermont History* (formerly the *Proceedings of the Vermont Historical Society* and *Vermont Quarterly*), which began in 1860.

The most complete work on Vermont local history remains Abby Hemenway's *Vermont Historical Gazetteer*, 5 volumes (1867-91), with its sections on Vermont towns. However, the entire state is not covered, and the work must be used with care. In addition to Hemenway, researchers at the Newberry will find a very good collection of local histories, both old and new. Since the town is the most important local government body in Vermont, most local histories are of towns rather than counties, although a few county histories do exist. Unlike Massachusetts, few Vermont towns have had their vital records published, but the Newberry has all of those that have appeared. Many were published in the *New England Historic Genealogical Register* and other periodicals. Vermont marriages through 1852 are available for Montpelier, Burlington, and Berlin. Some Vermont cemetery records have been transcribed, and again, they have appeared to a large extent in periodicals.

Local church history is a strength of the Newberry, and among the holdings for Vermont one will find many histories of individual congregations, and the *Minutes of the Annual Meeting of the General Convention of Congregational Ministers and Churches of Vermont*, 1st to 15th and 24th to 85th meeting (1795-1810, 1819-80, a few are missing), and the *Journal of the Annual Convention of the Protestant Episcopal Church, Vermont Diocese*, 42nd to 96th meetings (1832-86). These contain reports on the state of religion, lists of clergy, and reports from individual congregations.

Bibliographies and Guides

Committee for a New England Bibliography. *Vermont: A Bibliography of its History*, 1981. Excellent. Much of the material cited will be found at the Newberry.

Edward W. Hanson. "Vermont Genealogy: A Study in Migration." *New England Historic Genealogical Register* 133 (1979): 3-19. Very good. Reprinted in *Genealogical Research in New England*, Ralph J. Crandall, ed., 1984.

CHAPTER 12

THE MID-ATLANTIC

The Newberry Library holdings for the Mid-Atlantic states are generally good to very good and are particularly strong for the colonial and revolutionary periods. Unlike New England, little material of a collective or regional nature has been produced on the Mid-Atlantic states. In addition to a good collection of published colonial and early statehood records, the library also has description and travel accounts and works on boundaries and boundary disputes. The holdings of genealogical source material are also very good.

A large number of historical and genealogical periodicals are available, including many local journals. Local history holdings are uneven-- good or very good for Maryland, New Jersey, New York, and Pennsylvania, but much weaker for Delaware and the District of Columbia. Researchers working on the Mid-Atlantic states should be especially alert to check surrounding states for relevant material. For example, much Delaware material can be found in works on Pennsylvania and New York, and much New Jersey material can be found in New York sources.

DELAWARE

Delaware, one of the smallest states in the Union, is represented at the Newberry by a rather small collection of local and family history materials. Many important items on Delaware history are found in works on Pennsylvania and New York. Two typical examples are "Officers of the Colonies on the Delaware, 1614-1681," found in series 2 of the *Pen-*

nsylvania Archives; and material on the Dutch on the Delaware found in *Documents Relative to the Colonial History of the State of New York,* 15 volumes (1853-87).

The Newberry does have a very good collection of published state and colonial government records including various volumes of minutes of the House of Assembly; some votes and proceedings of the House of Representatives; *Governor's Register* (1926), which is an incomplete list of appointments made by executive authority, 1776-1851; *Minutes of the Council of the Delaware State From 1776-1792* (1887); *Original Land Titles in Delaware Commonly Known as the Duke of York Record* (1903); and *Land Survey Register, 1675-1679, West Side Delaware River, From Newcastle County, Delaware, into Bucks County, Pennsylvania* (1955).

The *Papers of the Historical Society of Delaware* are very useful. They include biographies, memoirs, diaries and journals, church records, and local, political, and military history. The first series appeared between 1879 and 1922 in sixty-seven volumes; the new series, in three volumes, appeared between 1927 and 1940. The *Delaware Archives,* 5 volumes (1911-16), is made up entirely of records of military service from the colonial period to 1827.

The library's holdings of local histories are small and undistinguished, as are the holdings of genealogical source material. However, seventeenth- and eighteenth-century wills and probate records are well documented in several printed sources.

Bibliographies and Guides
Henry Clay Reed and Marion B. Reed. *A Bibliography of Delaware Through 1960,* 1966. Not annotated and arrangement within subject sections is rather haphazard.

Periodical and Serial Publications
Delaware Genealogical Society Journal, 1980 to date.

The Delaware Historical and Genealogical Recall. 1 vol. (all published), 1933.

Delaware History, 1946 to date.

The Delaware Register and Farmers' Magazine. 2 vols., 1838-39.

The Maryland and Delaware Genealogist, 1959 to date.

DISTRICT OF COLUMBIA

The District of Columbia is coterminous with the city of Washington, the capital of the United States. Although the site was chosen by Congress in 1790, it was not until 1800 that government operations were moved to Washington. Researchers should check Card Catalogue entries under both "Washington, D. C.," and "District of Columbia." Land was ceded from Maryland and Virginia to establish the District of Columbia, therefore the records of Montgomery County, Maryland; Prince George County, Maryland; and Fairfax County, Virginia, may contain information on the District up through the first several years of the nineteenth century.

The best single source of local history information on the District of Columbia is *Columbia Historical Society Records* (1897+), which contains much neighborhood history. Homer A. Walker compiled *Historical Court Records of Washington, District of Columbia: Death Records of Washington, D. C., 1801-1878, as Taken From Administration of Estates...* (1955), and fourteen volumes of *Historical Court Records of Washington, District of Columbia: Marriages* (1955-56), which cover the years 1811 to 1858. Marriages and deaths from the newspaper *National Intelligencer* have been abstracted for the years 1800-50 and published as Special Publication Number 41 (1976) of the National Genealogical Society. Also available are the Mortality Schedules for the census years 1850-80.

Several microfilm compilations from the National Archives that deal with blacks in the District of Columbia are now at the library. These are Freedmen's Bureau Field Office Records; Records of the U. S. District Court for the District of Columbia Relating to Slaves, 1851-63, which includes manumissions, habeas corpus claims, and fugitive slave claims; and Records of the Board of Commissioners for the Emancipation of Slaves in the District of Columbia, 1862-63.

The Newberry Library does not have a particularly strong collection of histories of the District of Columbia and Washington, although there is a good deal of material on the capture of Washington by the British in 1814, much information on churches, many nineteenth-century guidebooks and descriptive accounts of the District, and many works on social life.

Bibliographies and Guides

June Andrew Babbel. *Lest We Forget, A Guide to Genealogical Research in the Nation's Capital,* 1976. Contains a small section on sources of information on District residents.

Wilhelmus Bogart Bryan. *Bibliography of the District of Columbia,* 1900.

Perry G. Fisher. *Materials for the Study of Washington: A Selected Annotated Bibliography,* 1974. Contains books and pamphlets. Annotations are lengthy, interesting, and useful.

MARYLAND

Interest in state and local history has been very strong in Maryland, evidenced by the large number of books and articles written over the years. A very good selection of these will be found at The Newberry Library.

The Maryland Historical Society has been a prolific publisher of works on Maryland history, nearly all of which are part of the Newberry collection. These include *Publications of the Maryland Historical Society* (1844-96); the Maryland Historical Society Fund Publications, 38 volumes (1867-1901); and the most important series for local and family historians, *Archives of Maryland,* which began in 1883 and now numbers over seventy volumes. The *Archives of Maryland* includes many colonial and early state records such as Revolutionary War muster rolls, proceedings of the Provincial Court, proceedings and acts of the Assembly, and some county court proceedings.

The library has several series and sets which researchers may find helpful. These include many volumes in the Johns Hopkins Studies in Historical and Political Science (1882+); *Reports of the Society for the History of the Germans in Maryland,* 32 volumes (1887-1966); *Maryland Genealogies* (1980), a consolidation of articles from the *Maryland Historical Magazine*; Maryland Bicentennial Studies series, 5 volumes (1973-77); and *Publications of the Thomas Bray Club,* 7 volumes (1916), which reprinted rare works on religion and Maryland. The Newberry also has all the Thomas Bray Club reprints in the original editions.

A very good collection of local histories, description and travel accounts, and compilations of local records will be found at the Newberry. These include rare early descriptive accounts such as *A Relation of Maryland; Together, With a Map of the Country, the Conditions of Plantation, His Majesties Charter to the Lord Baltemore,* a promotional tract published in 1635; and *A Character of the Province of Maryland* (1666) by George Alsop, an indentured servant. This was one of the earliest descriptions of life in Maryland. The collection also contains several indexes to vital records in newspapers, a large number of church records, a good deal on Maryland boundary disputes, some material on the Germans in Maryland, good periodical holdings, and colonial Maryland wills, which are well covered in several publications.

Bibliographies and Guides

Mary Keysor Meyer. *Genealogical Research in Maryland: A   Guide.* 3rd ed., 1983. A very good guide, of value to   genealogists and local historians. Contains a bibliography of printed sources by county.

Eleanor Phillips Passano. *An Index of the Source Records of Maryland,* 1940. Dated, but still useful. Includes archival and manuscript sources as well as printed materials. Topics covered include surnames, counties, and church records.

Periodical and Serial Publications

Chronicles of St. Mary's, 1953 to date.

The County Court Note-Book; A Little Bulletin of History and Genealogy. 10 vols., 1921-31.

The Maryland and Delaware Genealogist, 1959 to date.

The Maryland Genealogical Society Bulletin, 1960 to date.

The Maryland Historical and Genealogical Bulletin. 21 vols., 1930-50.

Maryland Historical Magazine, 1906 to date.

Maryland Magazine of Genealogy, 1978 to date.

Bulletin of the Maryland Original Research Society of Baltimore. 3 vols., 1906-13.

Western Maryland Genealogy, 1985 to date.

NEW JERSEY

Despite the destruction of many early New Jersey records (no census returns exist, for example, until 1830), there are a great many valuable New Jersey local history and genealogy sources in print, and researchers will find a very good collection of them at the Newberry.

The most important printed source on the early history of New Jersey is the multi-volume series known as the *New Jersey Archives.* Series 1, *Documents Relating to the Colonial, Revolutionary and Post-Revolutionary History of the State of New Jersey* (1880-1949), contains forty-two volumes of wills, colonial documents, extracts from newspapers, marriage records, and journals of the Council of New Jersey. Series 2, *Documents Relating to the Revolutionary History of the State of New Jersey* (1901-17), has five volumes, and a third series began publication in 1974. A complete set of the *Archives* is available at the Newberry.

A great deal of New Jersey material will also be found in publications from adjoining states. For example, volume 12 of *Documents Relative to the Colonial History of the State of New York* (1877) has material on the English, Dutch, and Swedish settlements in West Jersey, and *The Pennsylvania Magazine of History and Biography* contains many articles on New Jersey. Another useful documentary source is *Minutes of the Board of General Proprietors of the Eastern Division of New Jersey, 1685-1794,* 4 volumes (1949-85). This set contains a great deal on trade, industry, boundary disputes, quit rents, petitions for grants of land, and the ordering of warrants for surveys. The minutes of the Western Division have not appeared in print. Many more New Jersey colonial and revolutionary documents are in print, and most will be found at the library.

The Newberry collection holds many rare and important early works including the first history of the state, Samuel Smith's *The History of the Colony of Nova-Caesaria, or New Jersey...to the Year 1721* (1765); *The Grants, Concessions, and Original Constitutions of the Province of New Jersey...* (1758); and *An Historical and Geographical Account of the Province and Country of Pensilvania; and of West-New-Jersey in America* (1698), by Gabriel Thomas, one of the earliest accounts of this area, written to encourage colonization.

A very good collection of local histories for New Jersey will be found at the Newberry, as well as a number of transcriptions and indexes to marriages, probate and land records, a very good collection of description and travel accounts, and many New Jersey historical and genealogical periodicals. These include all the marriage records published by H. Stanley Craig, and many, but not all, of the South Jersey publications he issued. A good deal of local history is contained in *Historical Collections of the State of New Jersey* by John Warner Barber and Henry Howe, a very popular work which appeared in several editions in the nineteenth century (first edition, 1841). Two other historical series which will be found at the library are *Collections of the New Jersey Historical Society* (1846+), which presently numbers seventeen volumes; and the New Jersey Historical Series, 27 volumes plus 2 supplements (1964-65), of which the Newberry lacks a few volumes.

Bibliographies and Guides

Nelson R. Burr. *A Narrative and Descriptive Bibliography of New Jersey,* 1964. Excellent work including both books and periodical articles.

Doris M. Perry. *This is New Jersey, A Tercentenary Bibliography,* 1963. Annotated guide to holdings at the Trenton State University library. Good for Trenton and Mercer County.

Kenn Stryker-Rodda. *New Jersey: Digging for Ancestors in the Garden State,* 1970. Very good. Bibliographies will be useful to local historians as well as genealogists.

Periodical and Serial Publications

Papers and Proceedings of the Bergen County Historical Society. 15 vols., 1902-22.

Bergen County History, 1970-77. An annual publication.

The Cape May County, New Jersey Magazine, 1931 to date.

The Genealogical Magazine of New Jersey, 1925 to date.

Bulletin of the Gloucester County Historical Society, 1947 to date.

The Jerseyman. 11 vols., 1891-1905.

New Jersey Genesis. 20 vols., 1953-73.

Proceedings of the New Jersey Historical Society. 84 vols. in 4 series, 1845-1966. Continued as *New Jersey History,* 1967 to date.

Somerset County Historical Quarterly. 8 vols., 1912-19.

South Jersey Magazine, 1972 to date.

The Vineland Historical Magazine. 54 vols., 1916-78.

NEW YORK

The state of New York is of great interest and importance to many local historians and genealogists because its network of roads, canals, and railways made New York the primary gateway to the Middle West and West from the Mid-Atlantic and New England states.

The Newberry Library has a very large collection on New York, which is strongest for the colonial and revolutionary periods. Numerous colonial and revolutionary records have been published by a variety of individuals and organizations. Probably the best known work is *Documents Relative to the Colonial History of the State of New York,* 15 volumes (1853-87), edited by Edmund B. O'Callaghan. O'Callaghan also compiled *Documentary History of the State of New York,* 4 volumes (1849-51); *History of New Netherlands* (1846-48); and *Calendar of New York Colonial Commissions, 1680-1770* (1929).

Collections of the New York Historical Society (1809+), contains much of interest on the colonial and revolutionary periods, including muster rolls and abstracts of wills in the Surrogate's Office, New York City. Berthold Fernow also compiled and edited much early documentary material on New York. His works include *The Records of New Amsterdam, From 1653 to 1674,* 7 volumes (1897); *Documents Relating to the History and Settlements of the Towns Along the Hudson and Mohawk Rivers (With the Exception of Albany), 1630 to 1684* (1881); plus volumes of early wills and military lists. Also important for the colonial period are the various volumes of *New York Historical Manuscripts: Dutch* and *New York Historical Manuscripts: English,* published under the auspices of the Holland Society of New York. The early records of *some* towns including Huntington, New Rochelle, North Hempstead, South Hempstead, Oyster Bay, and Jamaica, Long Island have also been published.

The library has a very good collection of local histories and description and travel accounts. Unlike Connecticut and Massachusetts, New York did not begin keeping vital statistics records until 1880 and, in some cases, as late as 1914. Thus church records take on added importance in this state. The Newberry has a strong collection on religion and churches in New York. These include denominational histories, biographical works, and a large collection of transcribed church records. Many of these have appeared in periodicals such as the *New York Genealogical and Biographical Record,* as well as in separate publications, such as the records of German churches in the Hudson Valley being done by Arthur C. M. Kelly.

Genealogists will find all the standard New York genealogical compendia by authors S. V. Talcott, Cuyler Reynolds, William R. Cutter, Janet W. Foley, and Margherita A. Hamm. A great deal of genealogical material collected and abstracted by the Daughters of the American Colonists in New York has been deposited at the Newberry. Some of it will be found through the Card Catalogue, and some through the Local and Family History Vertical File. There is material on several of the land companies which helped settle New York, especially the Holland Land Company. The library also has on microfilm the state census schedules for New York for 1855 (part), 1875 (part), 1905 (part) and 1925 (complete). Some information not found on Federal census schedules, such as county of birth (for New York births) is included on the state schedules. Many abstracts of vital records from newspapers have been done in New York, including Joseph Gavit's *American Deaths and Marriages, 1784-1829* (1976), a microfilm publication containing 60,000 entries mostly from newspapers in the Hudson and Mohawk River valleys, along with a few entries from Pittsfield, Massachusetts. Many early colonial wills have been abstracted or calendared, and abstracted court records, deeds, guardianships, and naturalizations are available for some counties.

NEW YORK CITY

Because New York City presents some special problems for the local historian and genealogist, some items which relate specifically to researching in New York City deserve specific mention. Rosalie F. Bailey's *Guide to Genealogical and Biographical Sources for New York City, 1783-1898* (1954) gives detailed information on both printed and documentary sources. Other useful works are *Dictionary Catalog of Materials on New York City* (1977), a three-volume set from the Research Libraries of the New York Public Library, and *The Iconography of Manhattan Island, 1498-1909* (1915-28), by Isaac Newton Phelps Stokes. This latter work, in six oversized volumes, consists of copies of original documents, maps, views, a chronology, and a fine bibliography of basic sources of New York City history. The Newberry Library has an excellent collection of New York City directories (complete from 1829-1933, with some earlier volumes) and the twenty-eight volumes of the *Manual of the Corporation Council of New York* (1841-70). These volumes, edited by David T. Valentine, and known as *Valentine's Manuals,* contain facts about the government, appendices of historical material, and many good prints and maps. The library's holdings are quite good for the colonial and revolutionary periods, and there is also some material on the city in the nineteenth century, including works on social conditions, poverty, and charitable work.

Bibliographies and Guides

Dorothy C. Barck. *Some References for Genealogical Searching in New York State,* 1960. Very good.

Florence Clint. *New York Area Key,* 1979.

G. Glyndon Cole, ed. *Historical Materials Relating to Northern New York: A Union Catalog,* 1968. Very good guide to materials on fourteen northern New York counties.

Loren Fay. *New York Genealogical Research Secrets.* 4th ed., 1983.

Charles A. Flagg and Judson T. Jennings. "Bibliography of New York Colonial History." *New York State Library Bulletin.* No. 56 (February 1901).

James D. Folts. *The Genesee Region, 1790 to the Present: A Guide to its History,* 1978.

Harold Nestler. *A Bibliography of New York State Communities: Counties, Towns, Villages,* 1968. Far from complete; does not include periodical articles.

Research and Publications in New York State History, 1968/69 to date.

South Central Research Library Council. *A Guide to Local Historical Material in the Libraries of South Central New York State,* 1976.

Kenn Stryker-Rodda and Herbert F. Seversmith. *Long Island Genealogical Source Material,* 1962. A very fine bibliography, of use to local historians as well as genealogists.

Periodical and Serial Publications

The Dutch Settlers Society of Albany Yearbook, 1924 to date.

Early Settlers of New York State, Their Ancestors and Descendants. 9 vols., 1934-42.

De Halve Maen, 1973 (vol. 48) to date.

Yearbook of the Holland Society of New York. 35 vols., 1887/88-1930/37.

New York Genealogical and Biographical Record, 1870 to date.

Collections of the New York Genealogical and Biographical Society, 1890 to date.

New York Historical Society Quarterly, 1917 to date.

New York History, 1919 to date.

Proceedings of the New York State Historical Association. 2nd-24th annual meetings, 1901-24.

Tree Talks (Central New York Genealogical Society), 1961 to date.

Periodical or serial publications are also available for the counties of Bronx, Cayuga, Chemung, Dutchess, Erie, Nassau, Oneida, Schoharie, Ulster, and Wyoming, and for the Columbia Valley, Long Island, the Mohawk Valley, the city of Rochester, and the Saratoga Valley.

PENNSYLVANIA

Pennsylvania, appropriately known as the Keystone State, sits geographically between North and South and the East and the Midwest, and has played a key role in American history. Researchers will find a very strong collection of Pennsylvania materials at The Newberry Library.

The single most important printed source for historical and genealogical research is the *Pennsylvania Archives* (1838-1935), which includes 119 volumes in nine series plus an initial series, *Colonial Records of Pennsylvania.* The *Pennsylvania Archives* includes lists of marriages, muster rolls, oaths of allegiance, church records, and many other documents and records of the colonial and commonwealth period. This set often overwhelms researchers; therefore, it is essential to consult some of the guides that have been prepared to assist users of the *Archives.* Three good guides are available: *Use of the Published Pennsylvania Archives in Genealogical Research* (1978) by Jean S. Morris, *Guide to the Published Archives of Pennsylvania...* (1949) by Martha L. Simonetti, and *Genealogical Research in the Published Pennsylvania Archives* (1974) by Sally A. Weikel.

The Newberry's holdings of local histories and items of genealogical interest are outstanding, although heavily weighted to the Colonial and Revolutionary periods. The library has works by important early Pennsylvania historians John Blair Linn, William H. Egle, and Israel D. Rupp, as well as a fine collection of more recently published local histories. Researchers will find a great many transcripts of church records, abstracts of genealogical information from newspapers, cemetery transcriptions, court, probate, and land records.

An interesting curiosity found among the library's Pennsylvania holdings is *The Horn Papers; Early Westward Movement on the Monongahela and Upper Ohio, 1765-1795* (1945), by William Franklin Horn. *The Horn Papers* is probably the most famous forgery ever uncovered in American local history. This work includes the diaries of Jacob and Christopher Horn, maps, court orders, an early court docket, and family histories of many early settlers in the region of southwest Pennsylvania, northwest Virginia and Maryland. Although some factual information was included, most of the material was fabricated. The exception is the maps in Volume 3 of Washington, Fayette, and Greene counties which are authentic and were copied from the Pennsylvania Land Office.[1]

Several important sources are available on seventeenth- and eighteenth-century Pennsylvania. The *1798 Direct Tax of Pennsylvania* on twenty-four reels of microfilm, names persons owning real property or slaves, locations and descriptions of dwellings, value of property, and taxes owed. This tax list, sometimes known as the Pennsylvania Glass or Window Tax, does contain the names of many individuals who do not appear in the 1800 Pennsylvania census schedules. *Records of the Provincial Council, 1682-1776* is available on twenty-six reels of microfilm. This microfilm set of the original manuscript records is partially indexed. Another useful source is the eleven volumes of *The Susquehanna Company Papers* (1930-71), edited by Julian P. Boyd and Robert J. Taylor. Under the auspices of the Susquehanna Company, people primarily from Connecticut settled in disputed parts of northeastern Pennsylvania beginning in 1753.

Some other important sources include *Pennsylvania Newspaper Excerpts,* three microfilm reels of "excerpts of genealogical interest abstracted from Pennsylvania newspapers in the collection of the Historical Society of Pennsylvania"; the *Pennsylvania State Manual,* 1881-1900 (scattered volumes) and 1902-29, which includes lists of post offices and biographies of state legislators; and two contemporary periodicals: *Hazard's Register of Pennsylvania, Devoted to the Preservation of Facts and Documents, And Every Kind of Useful Information Respecting the State of Pennsylvania,* 16 volumes (1828-35) and *The Olden Time; A Monthly Publication, Devoted to the Preservation of Documents and Other Authentic Information in Relation to the Early Explorations, and the Settlement and Improvement of the Country Around the Head of the Ohio...* (January 1846-December 1847).

Many researchers are seeking information on the Pennsylvania Germans, or Pennsylvania Dutch as they are often known, and the Newberry has a large collection of material on these people. To locate material in the Card Catalogue on Pennsylvania Germans, researchers must check under *two* different subject headings: "Germans in Pennsylvania" and "German Americans--Pennsylvania." The standard bibliography is still Emil Meynen's *Bibliography on German Settlements in Colonial North America, Especially on the Pennsylvania Germans and their Descendants, 1683-1933* (1937). The library has several serial and periodical publications, including *Pennsylvania German Society Quarterly* (formerly *Der Reggeboge,* 1967+); *The Penn Germania,* 15 volumes (1900-14); *Publications of the Pennsylvania German Folklore Society,* 28 volumes (1936-66), many volumes of which are of genealogical and historical interest; and *Proceedings and Addresses of the Pennsylvania German Society,* 63 volumes (1891-1966). These latter two publications merged to become

Publications of the Pennsylvania German Society (1968+).

Bibliographies and Guides

Raymond M. Bell. *Searching in Western Pennsylvania,* 1968.

John E. Bodnar. *Ethnic History of Pennsylvania: A Selected Bibliography,* 1974.

Florence Clint. *Pennsylvania Area Key.* 2nd ed., 1976. Helpful to beginning genealogical researchers.

Floyd C. Hoenstine. *Guide to Genealogical and Historical Research in Pennsylvania.* 4th ed., 1978, plus 1985 supplement. Lists over 2500 publications and includes a surname index which cites publications in which information on the surname can be found. Supplement includes 400 additional titles.

George K. Schweitzer. *Pennsylvania Genealogical Research,* 1986.

David E. Washburn. *The Peoples of Pennsylvania: An Annotated Bibliography of Resource Materials,* 1981.

Norman B. Wilkinson, comp. *Bibliography of Pennsylvania History.* 2nd ed., 1957. Excellent, comprehensive guide with brief annotations.

Carol Wall, comp. *Bibliography of Pennsylvania History: A Supplement,* 1976. These works are now continued by *Pennsylvania Historical Bibliography (1970+),* a triennial publication featuring sections on local history, church history, ethnic groups, and much more.

Periodical and Serial Publications

Memoirs of the Historical Society of Pennsylvania. 14 vols., 1864-95.

The Journal of Erie Studies, 1972 to date.

The Pennsylvania Genealogical Magazine, 1895 to date.

Pennsylvania History, 1934 to date.

The Pennsylvania Magazine of History and Biography, 1877 to date.

Western Pennsylvania Genealogical Quarterly, 1974 to date.

Western Pennsylvania Historical Magazine, 1918 to date.

Your Family Tree. 11 vols., 1948-64.

Periodical publications are also available on the counties of Berks, Bucks, Franklin, Lancaster, Lehigh, Lycoming, Mercer, Montgomery, Northampton, and York, and on the Wyoming Valley and Muncy.

NOTES

1. For further information on this remarkable forgery see Arthur Pierce Middleton and Douglass Adair, "The Mystery of the Horn Papers," *William and Mary Quarterly* ser. 3, vol. 4 (October 1947): 409-45.

CHAPTER 13

THE SOUTH

The scope and size of the Newberry's holdings on the Southern states varies greatly. Strong collections exist for Virginia and the Carolinas, for example, while the holdings for Alabama and Mississippi are weak. Many publications on one state contain valuable information on neighboring states. There is much information on South Carolina in published records of North Carolina and Georgia, and material on Mississippi and Alabama is frequently found together. Overall the collection is quite good for the early period of exploration and discovery, particularly for primary and secondary material on the period of Spanish exploration and settlement in the Gulf Coast states. A useful bibliography on this subject is William S. Coker's "Research in the Spanish Borderlands," *Latin American Research Review* 7 (Summer 1972): 3-94, which covers Alabama, Mississippi, Louisiana, and east and west Florida. The territorial period for those states outside the original colonies is also well covered, and relevant volumes of *The Territorial Papers of the United States* are important sources.

One of the library's overall strengths is its collection of description and travel accounts, and the holdings for the Southern states are no exception. Some useful bibliographies are Thomas D. Clark's *Travels in the Old South, A Bibliography* (1956-59) and *Travels in the New South, A Bibliography* (1962); and E. Merton Coulter's *Travels in the Confederate States, A Bibliography* (1948, reprinted 1961).

Researchers will find a good deal on land grants awarded by one state in another state or territory, state boundaries and boundary disputes, social life and customs, and extracts of vital records from newspapers. The library has all of the 1850 and 1870 Census Population Schedules for the southern and border states (and scattered holdings for 1860 and 1880), as well as all the 1850 and 1860 Slave Schedules. During the eighteenth and nineteenth centuries passports were issued for travel through various parts of the South. These passports are important historical and genealogical sources, and Dorothy W. Potter has compiled a comprehensive list of Indian, Spanish, and other land passports for Tennessee, Kentucky, Georgia, Mississippi, Virginia, and the Carolinas in *Passports of Southeastern Pioneers, 1770-1823* (1984).

The library is in the process of acquiring a number of records which will greatly strengthen its holdings on the ante-bellum South and blacks in the South. These include:

1. "Records of Ante-Bellum Southern Plantations from the Revolution Through the Civil War." This microfilm series includes diaries, family correspondence, plantation journals, farm books, crop books, overseers' journals, business papers, and slave lists.

2. "Index to Compiled Service Records for the United States Colored Troops." This ninety-eight-reel microfilm set is a name index to approximately 180,000 blacks who served in the Civil War. It lists not only blacks from the South, but also many free blacks from the North. The library does not have copies of the actual compiled service records from the National Archives.

3. "Freedmen's Savings and Trust Company Registers, 1865-1874." This microfilm set from the National Archives includes personal information on depositors.

4. "Indexes to Deposit Ledgers from the Freedmen's Savings and Trust Company, 1865-1874."

5. "Freedmen's Bureau Field Office Records." This set consists of records of ten states and the District of Columbia. Florida, Kentucky, and Maryland are not included. The genealogical value of these records varies from state to state. Records for some states, including Mississippi, Arkansas, and Louisiana, contain freedmen's marriage registers.

For genealogists, the library has all standard genealogical compendia including *Notable Southern Families,* 7 volumes (1918-40) by Zella Armstrong and *Historical Southern Families* (1957+) by John B. Boddie, both of which must be used with caution. Another useful source is E. Kay Kirkham's *An Index to Some of the Family Records of the Southern States: 35,000 Microfilm References From the NSDAR Files and Elsewhere* (1979). This is an index only, but may provide useful clues for further research.

Periodical and Serial Publications

Gulf States Historical Magazine, 1902-04.

Hispanic American Historical Review, 1918 to date.

Journal of Southern History, 1935 to date.

The Southern Genealogists Exchange Quarterly. 15 vols., 1958-74.

Southern Historical Publications. 19 vols., 1965-74.

Papers of the Southern Historical Society. 52 vols., 1876-1959.

Publications of the Southern History Association. 11 vols., 1897-1907.

ALABAMA

Alabama, along with several other states of the deep South, either belonged to, was part of, or was claimed by several countries, states, and territories before attaining statehood. Researchers must know that Alabama was at various times part of the empires of France, Spain, and England, was part of Mississippi Territory, and had sections of its land claimed by Georgia and South Carolina. References to Alabama local and family history must sometimes be sought in sources on these countries and states. An example of such a work is *The Minutes, Journals, and Acts of the General Assembly of British West Florida* (1979) by Robert B. Rea and Milo B. Howard, Jr., which deals heavily with Alabama and also includes material on the rest of the Gulf coastal area.

The Alabama holdings at the Newberry are among the smallest and weakest in the library. The collection is better for the pre-territorial period, since the Newberry has strong holdings on the discovery, exploration, and early settlement of the Gulf Coast. Neither the state of Alabama nor the Alabama Historical Society has ever published a "State Papers" series, "collections of the state historical society," or other comparable series.

Volumes 5, 6, and 18 of *The Territorial Papers of the United States* are very helpful and include names and information on many early settlers. The *American State Papers,* Public Lands Series, Class VIII, is also useful for early land claims and disputes. One of the largest and best known works on Alabama is the 245 volumes of *Alabama Records* compiled by Pauline Jones Gandrud and Kathleen Paul Jones. Unfortunately, the Newberry has only about a dozen of the volumes from this series. Two sources that can be found at the Newberry are the *Transactions of the Alabama Historical Society,* new series, volumes 2-5 (volume 1 was never published) (1897/98-1904) and *Alabama Official and Statistical Register.* The library has eight volumes of the *Register* between 1903 and 1927, which contain lists of government officials and some lengthy biographies.

The collection of Alabama local histories is small and spotty, and there are few transcriptions or indexes of vital records, cemetery listings, probates, and other sources of genealogical interest. One exception is the series *Alabama Soldiers* (1975+) by Pauline Jones Gandrud which covers the Revolutionary War, War of 1812, and Indian Wars. The records of several federal land offices in Alabama are also available:

Old Cahaba, Old St. Stephens, Old Tuskaloosa, and Old Sparta and Elba.

Bibliographies and Guides

Leah Rawls Atkins. *A Manual for Writing Alabama State and Local History,* 1976. Very basic guide for beginners. "Bibliographical Essay on Alabama History" may be useful.

Thomas M. Owen. *A Bibliography of Alabama,* 1897.

Periodical and Serial Publications

AGE (Alabama Genealogical Exchange), 1984 to date.

Alabama Genealogical Register. 10 vols., 1959-68.

The Alabama Historical Quarterly, 1956 (vol. 18) to date.

The Alabama Review: A Quarterly Journal of Alabama History, 1948 to date (Newberry lacks vols. 22-25).

North Alabama Historical Association Bulletin. 6 vols., 1956-61.

ARKANSAS

The Arkansas holdings at The Newberry Library, while far from strong, are among the best for the deep Southern states. Some guides and bibliographies exist, and the library has runs of several local historical society periodicals, a modest collection of local histories and genealogical source material, and a good collection of works on the Civil War in Arkansas.

For the territorial period, volumes 19, 20, and 21 of *The Territorial Papers of the United States* are essential. The Newberry has approximately half of the published local and county histories on Arkansas, including the Goodspeed Histories. Some transcriptions and indexes to marriage records are available at the library, including several volumes of county marriages by Bobbie J. McLane. Few other examples of genealogical source material will be found. The library does have printed indexes to the Arkansas Mortality Schedules for the census years 1850-80, as well as the microfilm copies. Press Argus of Van Buren, Arkansas, has published to date sixteen volumes in its Arkansas Historical Series; the Newberry lacks volumes 1 and 12.

One of the most important Arkansas sources at the Newberry is the lengthy run of the *Arkansas Gazette,* one of the most influential newspapers in the West. The library's holdings begin with the first issue, 20 November 1819, and go to 1 December 1875, with only a few missing issues. This newspaper did have significance beyond the borders of Arkansas, and since it has been indexed, it should definitely be consulted by researchers working in this area of the South.

Bibliographies and Guides

Georgia H. Clark and R. Bruce Parham. "Arkansas County and Local Histories: A Bibliography." *The Arkansas Historical Quarterly* 36 (Spring 1977): 50-84. Good.

Tom W. Dillard and Valerie Thwing. *Researching Arkansas History: A Beginners Guide,* 1979. Includes an annotated bibliography.

Larry S. Perry. *Arkansas Genealogy Bibliography,* 1977. Good.

Periodical and Serial Publications

The Arkansas Historical Quarterly, 1942 to date.

Faulkner Facts and Fiddlings (Faulkner County). 21 vols., 1959-79.

Independence County Chronicle, 1959 to date.

Pope County Historical Association Quarterly, 1966 to date.

The Record (Hot Springs-Garland County Historical Society), 1960 to date.

White County Heritage. 14 vols., 1962-1976.

FLORIDA

The area now encompassing the state of Florida has had a long, rich, and varied history, having at times been part of the empires of Spain and Britain before becoming a part of the United States in 1821. The Newberry's holdings are excellent for works on the discovery and exploration period. Researchers will find much on Spanish Florida and the French settlements of the sixteenth century. The nineteenth century is not covered in great detail, although there is some promotional and description and travel literature for the nineteenth and early twentieth centuries. The library has a small collection of local histories, but little genealogical source material. In 1885, with federal assistance, a special state census was taken in Florida. The population, mortality, agricultural, and manufacturing schedules are available on microfilm. Also available are selected volumes of the series Florida State University Studies, some of which deal with state and local history.

The Newberry's many works on the exploration and settlement of Florida include such rare and significant items as *Historia de la Fundacion y Discurso de la Prouincia de Santiago de Mexico...* (1596) by the Archbishop of Santiago, Agustin Davila Padilla, which is an account of Tristan de Luna's 1559 attempt to settle in the Gulf Region; *Ensayo Cronologico, Para la Historia General de la Florida* (1723), by Andres Gonzalez de Barcia Carballido y Zuniga; and Denys Rolle's account of a colony in Florida, *To the Right Honourable the Lords of His Majesty's*

Most Honourable Privy Council, the Humble Petition of Denys Rolle...Setting Forth the Hardships, Inconveniencies, and Grievances Which Have Attended Him in His Attempts to Make a Settlement in East Florida... (1766).

Several collections of documents will be of use to researchers. The eleven volumes of publications of the Florida State Historical Society (1922-33) include *Colonial Records of Spanish Florida.* All three series of Benjamin Franklin French's *Historical Collections of Louisiana and Florida* (1846-53, 1869, 1875) are at the Newberry. French's work contains transcripts of original documents on exploration and settlement, biographies, historical notes, memoirs, and journals. The library also has some works on Spanish Florida published in Spain such as *Documentos Historicos de la Florida y la Luisiana* (1912), edited by Manuel Serrano y Sanz.

For the territorial period (1821-45), volumes 22-26 of *The Territorial Papers of the United States* include not only records and correspondence of territorial officials, but also many petitions and letters signed by Florida residents. The library also has the early newspaper *Florida Argus* for 1828.

Bibliographies and Guides

Michael H. Harris. *Florida History: A Bibliography,* 1972. Includes books, articles, theses, and dissertations. Good.

James A. Servies. *A Bibliography of West Florida.* Rev. ed., 3 vols. plus supplement, 1978. Good.

Periodical and Serial Publications

Apalachee (Tallahassee Historical Society), 1944 to date.

El Escribano (St. Augustine Historical Society annual), 1959 (number 30) to date.

Florida Historical Quarterly, 1908 to date.

Jacksonville Genealogical Society Quarterly, 1973 to date.

Tallahassee Historical Society Annual, 1934-39.

Tequesta (Historical Association of Southern Florida), 1941 to date.

GEORGIA

Georgia, the largest of the thirteen colonies, has been the subject of much state, local, and family history written over the years. The Newberry has a fine collection of the writings of prominent Georgia historians from Rev. Alexander Hewatt, whose *An Historical Account of the Rise and Progress of the Colonies of South Carolina and Georgia* (1779) was the first history of the state, through the works of Hugh McCall,

George White, Absalom Harris Chappell, E. Merton Coulter, and Kenneth Coleman.

A number of compilations of records and serial publications are available at The Newberry Library. One of the most important is *The Colonial Records of the State of Georgia*, volumes 1-19, 21-26 (1904-16). They contain the papers and correspondence of the Trustees for the establishment of the colony of Georgia, including material on James Oglethorpe; journals of various legislative bodies; and the proceedings and minutes of the Governor and Council. The Newberry also has volumes 20, and 27-39 of *The Colonial Records of the State of Georgia* on ten reels of microfilm. These volumes contain unpublished colonial records copied from the British Public Record Office and are now being edited and published by the University of Georgia Press.

Other official record compilations include *The Revolutionary Records of the State of Georgia*, 3 volumes (1908) and *The Confederate Records of the State of Georgia*, volumes 1-4 and 6 (volume 5 was never published) (1909-11). Some other important series are *Collections of the Georgia Historical Society* (1840+), which presently numbers twenty volumes; *Pioneers of Wiregrass Georgia*, 7 volumes plus index (1951-79), by Folks Huxford, which contains material on several southeastern Georgia counties; and the *Colonial Records Series* (1975+), published by the R. J. Taylor Foundation, which transcribes conveyance books, probate records, and other colonial sources.

Family historians and those interested in Georgia biography should consult *The Leon S. Hollingsworth Genealogical Card File* (1979), available at the library on three microfilm reels. This file contains approximately 45,000 references to individuals and families. Although the material deals primarily with Georgians, there are some references to individuals and families in the Carolinas, Virginia, and Alabama.

Land grants and land records are very important in Georgia local history. Three kinds of land grants are found: headrights, bounty lands, and lottery grants. Six land lotteries were held between 1805 and 1832, and the Newberry has all the published works on these land lotteries, which generally include the names of the winners. Other important land grant sources are *Index to the Headright and Bounty Grants of Georgia, 1756-1909* (1970) by Silas E. Lucas and *English Crown Grants in Georgia, 1755-1775*, 9 volumes (1972-74).

The Newberry's Georgia holdings are strongest for the period before and during the Civil War. The collection of local histories is good, and there is good material on description and travel and social life and customs. Georgia wills and probate records are documented in a number of sources. In addition to transcripts of probate records from individual counties, several statewide compilations exist: *Index to Probate Records of Colonial Georgia, 1733-1778* (1983), edited by Marilyn L. Adams; *Abstracts of the Colonial Wills...1733-1777* (1962), compiled by the Georgia Chapter, National Society Colonial Dames of

America; *Index to Georgia Wills, 1777-1924* (1976, reprinted 1985), edited by Jeannette Holland Austin; and *Georgia Wills 1733-1860* (1976), by Ted O. Brooke. Cemetery and marriage records are available for many areas. Joseph T. Maddox, for one, has published several volumes of early Georgia marriages. The Newberry also has the Mortality Schedules for the census years 1850-80.

Bibliographies and Guides

Marilyn Adams. *Georgia Local and Family History Sources in Print,* 1982. Information on ordering in-print books.

Catalogue of the Wymberley Jones de Renne Georgia Library. 3 vols., 1931. Very good for pre-1900 materials.

Robert Scott Davis, Jr. *Research in Georgia,* 1981. Very good section on land lotteries, plus a fine bibliography of printed works.

_____. *A Researcher's Library of Georgia History, Genealogy, and Records Sources,* 1985.

James E. Dorsey. *Georgia Genealogy and Local History: A Bibliography,* 1983. Very good.

Arthur Ray Rowland and James E. Dorsey. *A Bibliography of the Writings on Georgia History, 1900-1970,* 1978, plus 1983 supplement. Very good.

John Eddins Simpson. *Georgia History: A Bibliography,* 1976. Not annotated, but has good chapters on family and local history.

Periodical and Serial Publications

The Atlanta Historical Journal, 1927 to date.

Georgia Genealogical Magazine, 1961 to date.

The Georgia Genealogist. 52 numbers, 1969-84.

Georgia Historical Quarterly, 1917 to date.

Richmond County History, 1969 to date.

KENTUCKY

Researchers will find a wealth of material at The Newberry Library on Kentucky, the first state west of the Appalachian Mountains to be admitted to the Union. Included in the holdings are a number of rare works: John Filson's *The Discovery, Settlement and Present State of Kentucke...* (1784), considered to be one of the most significant American books published in the eighteenth century--it contained the first biographical sketch of Daniel Boone; the first issue of the first edition of Filson's *This Map of Kentucke...* (1784); one of the earliest histories of

Kentucky, Humphrey Marshall's *The History of Kentucky* (1812); *An Account of the Remarkable Occurrences in the Life and Travels of Col. James Smith,* an Indian captivity narrative published in 1799; and the first history of Louisville, Henry M'Murtrie's *Sketches of Louisville and Its Environs* (1819).

One of the most important sources for the early history of Kentucky is the thirty-six volumes of the *Publications of the Filson Club* (1884-1938). Included among the publications are Willard Rouse Jillson's *Old Kentucky Entries and Deeds* (1926), *The Kentucky Land Grants* (1925), and James R. Robertson's *Petitions of the Early Inhabitants of Kentucky to the General Assembly of Virginia, 1769 to 1792* (1914). Researchers need to remember that prior to 1792, Kentucky was part of Virginia. Another important source is the Kentucky Papers in the Lyman C. Draper Manuscripts, which the Newberry has on microfilm. Mabel C. Weaks compiled the *Calendar of the Kentucky Papers of the Draper Collection of Manuscripts* (1925). This is not an every-name index to the Kentucky Papers, but a calendar of the Papers in volumes 11-19 and 26-30 of the Draper collection. See Chapter 10 for more information on the Lyman C. Draper Manuscripts.

The Newberry has a good collection of local histories, and the collection is very good for more recently published works. W. H. Perrin's *Kentucky, A History of the State* (1885-88), which appeared in several editions, contains hundreds of biographical sketches and is available at the library. Another useful state and local history series is the forty-one volumes of The Kentucky Bicentennial Bookshelf (1974-79), published by the University Press of Kentucky. Researchers will also find the Mortality Schedules for the census years 1850-80, and all pre-1860 directories.

The library has a very good collection of transcriptions of vital records, probates, deeds, tax records, court order books, cemetery records, and minute books for Kentucky counties. For wills, researchers should consult *Index to Kentucky Wills to 1851: the Testators* (1977) by Ronald Vern Jackson. A number of works deal with early land grants and land records in Kentucky, including the volumes by Willard Rouse Jillson mentioned above and *Master Index Virginia Surveys and Grants, 1774-1791* (1976) by Joan E. Brookes-Smith. This latter work covers lands granted by Virginia in Kentucky for service against the French and Indians. *Kentucky Genealogical Index* (volume I, 1985) by Glenda K. Trapp and Michael L. Cook, is an every-name index through 1980 to four Kentucky periodicals. The Newberry has all four publications: *Kentucky Ancestors, Kentucky Genealogist, Kentucky Pioneer Genealogy and Records,* and *The East Kentuckian.* All publications by noted Kentucky researchers such as J. Estelle Stewart King, Julia Spencer Ardery, Ednah McAdams, Willard Rouse Jillson, and John Frederick Dorman will be found at the library. The library also has a very large collection of the compilations of pension, military, census, and other records done by Annie Burns Bell.

Bibliographies and Guides

John Winston Coleman. *A Bibliography of Kentucky History*, 1949. Very good, annotated.

Anne Hamilton. *Inside Kentucky: Containing a Bibliography of Source Materials on Kentucky*, 1974. Oriented to school librarians; has useful section "Kentucky History: Secondary Sources for Secondary Schools."

Beverly West Hathaway. *Kentucky Genealogical Research Sources*, 1974.

Willard Rouse Jillson. *Kentucky History: A Check and Finding List of the Principal Published and Manuscript Sources of the General, Regional, and County History of the Commonwealth, 1729-1936*, 1936. Good.

George K. Schweitzer. *Kentucky Genealogical Research*, 1983. Good.

Periodical and Serial Publications

Daviess County Historical Quarterly, 1983 to date.

The East Kentuckian: A Journal of History and Genealogy. 9 vols., 1965-73.

The Filson Club History Quarterly, 1926 to date.

Publications of the Filson Club. 36 vols., 1884-1938.

Kentucky Ancestors, 1965 to date.

The Kentucky Genealogist, 1959 to date.

Kentucky Genealogy and Biography, 1970 to date.

Kentucky Pioneer Genealogy and Records, 1979 to date.

Register of the Kentucky Historical Society, 1903 to date.

South Central Kentucky Historical and Genealogical Quarterly, 1973 to date.

LOUISIANA

The Newberry Library's holdings on Louisiana, while far from outstanding, are among the strongest for the Gulf Coast states. The collection is best for the pre-statehood period and contains little for the post-Civil War era. A number of important sources are available on the French and Spanish periods. *Records and Deliberations of the Cabildo, 1769-1803*, "A Record of Spanish Government in New Orleans," is available on microfilm with transcripts in both Spanish and English. Another useful source is *The Favrot Papers* (1940+), which presently covers the years 1695-1817. This work, begun by the Historical Records Survey, deals with a family that played an important role in Louisiana history. The first permanent settlement in Louisiana was at Natchitoches in 1714, and many of its early extant records have been published and are found at the library. The Newberry also has a number of transcriptions of early Catholic Church records including the Diocese of Baton Rouge, St. Louis Cathedral in New Orleans, and some Acadian churches. A number of works are available on the Acadians in Louisiana. The *Proceedings of the French Colonial Historical Society* (1976+) also includes articles on the state.

Louisiana is fortunate to have several very active, prolific compilers and editors of local historical and genealogical material. The Newberry has collected nearly all works by authors Winston DeVille, Elizabeth Shown Mills, and Donald J. Hebert. The latter's works include *Southwest Louisiana Records: Church and Civil Records of Settlers*, 33 volumes to date (1974+), covering 1756 to the early twentieth century, and *South Louisiana Records*, 12 volumes (1978-85). The library also has all three series of Benjamin Franklin French's *Historical Collections of Louisiana and Florida* (1846-53, 1869, 1875), which contain much description and travel information, transcripts of original documents, biographies, historical notes, memoirs and journals.

For information on Louisiana as a territory, volumes 9, 13, 14, and 15 of *The Territorial Papers of the United States* are very important. A small collection of genealogical source material is available, including twenty-one volumes of parish (county) records for the parishes of Iberville, Jefferson, and St. Barnard, transcribed by the Historical Records Survey. These include minutes of the Police Jury, a local governing body. The library has the Louisiana Mortality Schedules for the census years 1850-80 on microfilm. Two other series which may assist local and family historians are *Publications of the Louisiana Historical Society*, 10 volumes (1895-1917) and the Louisiana State University Studies Series (1931-41) which includes several volumes on state and local history.

Bibliographies and Guides

Glenn R. Conrad and Carl A. Brasseaux. *A Selected Bibliography of Scholarly Literature on Colonial Louisiana and New France*, 1982. Good but not annotated.

Light Townsend Cummins and Glen Jeansonne. *A Guide to the History of Louisiana*, 1982. Very good historiographical essays and descriptions of archival repositories.

Jack D. L. Holmes. *A Guide to Spanish Louisiana, 1762-1806,* 1970.

The Louisiana Union Catalog, 1959, plus supplements 1963+. Books about Louisiana and by Louisiana authors.

Periodical and Serial Publications

The Attakapas Gazette, 1966 to date.

The Louisiana Genealogical Register, 1954 to date.

Louisiana Historical Quarterly, 1917 to date.

Louisiana History, 1968 (vol. 9) to date.

New Orleans Genesis, 1962 to date.

Southern Studies, 1962 to date.

MISSISSIPPI

The Newberry Library's holdings on Mississippi are quite weak. Most basic source materials are available, but there are gaps, and the holdings of local histories and genealogical source material are quite slim.

Much of the Newberry's Mississippi holdings deal with its colonial and territorial periods. The library does have *Mississippi Provincial Archives: French Domination,* 5 volumes (1927-84); *Mississippi Provincial Archives: English Domination* (1911); and *The Mississippi Territorial Archives, 1798-1803* (1905). Volumes 5 and 6 of *The Territorial Papers of the United States* are very important sources on early nineteenth-century Mississippi.

Dunbar Rowland's *Mississippi, Comprising Sketches of Counties, Towns, Events, Institutions, and Persons, Arranged in Cyclopedic Form,* 4 volumes (1907), remains a useful reference work and a source of much biographical information. Other sources that may aid researchers include *Publications of the Mississippi Historical Society,* 1st series, 14 volumes (1898-1914) and "Centenary Series," 5 volumes (1916-25); and *The Official and Statistical Register of the State of Mississippi* compiled by Dunbar Rowland. The library has four volumes (1908, 1917, 1920/24, and 1924/28) which contain much historical, biographical, and genealogical information, and material on state institutions and government offices.

For those seeking information on blacks in Mississippi, the Newberry does have the Freedmen's Bureau Field Office Records on microfilm. The Mississippi records are among the best in terms of personal information about individuals. See the introductory remarks to this chapter for further information on these records.

Bibliographies and Guides

Mississippi Library Commission. *Mississippiana,* 1971. Works by and about Mississippi and Mississippians; contains much historical material.

Thomas M. Owen. *A Bibliography of Mississippi,* 1899.

Periodical and Serial Publications

The Journal of Mississippi History, 1939 to date.

Mississippi Cemetery and Bible Records (Mississippi Genealogical Society), 1954 to date.

Mississippi Genealogy and Local History. 2 vols., 1969-70.

Northeast Mississippi Historical Journal. 6 vols., 1967-74.

NORTH CAROLINA

There is a wealth of printed and published material available for the local and family historian of North Carolina. The North Carolina Division of Archives and History has been extremely active for many years in publishing state and colonial documents and papers of prominent North Carolinians. In addition, in recent years there has been a great deal of interest in North Carolina local and family history at the grassroots level, in community colleges, and local historical and genealogical societies. This interest has generated increased publications in the field.

Several series and serial publications are important sources of information. One of the most important works is *The Colonial Records of North Carolina* and *The State Records of North Carolina,* 26 volumes (1886-1907), which include legislative journals, tax lists, newspaper extracts, letters of governors and many other official documents. A new series of *The Colonial Records of North Carolina* began in 1963. The North Carolina Historical Commission published thirty volumes of *Publications of the North Carolina Historical Commission* (1908-69), which are available at the Newberry. Included in the *Publications* are eleven volumes of *Records of the Moravians in North Carolina,* covering the period 1752-1879, plus other works on the early exploration and settlement of the state. Two other historical series found at the library are *James Sprunt Historical Studies,* over fifty volumes to date (1900+) and *Trinity College Historical Society Papers,* 32 volumes (1897-1956).

The Newberry's holdings of local histories are fair to good. The collection is best for works published in the last twenty years. The collection is very good for collective biographies, including the new, scholarly *Dictionary of North Carolina Biography* (1979+); description and travel accounts; and works on the early settlement of North Carolina. One example of an early promotional tract, and the first real history of the state is *Virgo Triumphans: or, Virginia Richly and Truly Valued; More Especially the South Part Thereof: viz. the Fertile Carolana, and No Lesse Excellent Isle of Roanoak,...* (1650), by Edward Williams, Gentleman.

A very good collection of transcribed state, county, and local government records will be found. One of the most significant items is

An Index to Marriage Bonds Filed in the North Carolina State Archives (1977). This microfiche set includes approximately 170,000 marriage bonds filed throughout the state between 1741 and 1868. There is both a bride and groom index. Many pre-1800 wills and inventories have been abstracted by J. Bryan Grimes and others, but the abstracts are often incomplete. Nearly all colonial grants for land patents have been published in abstract form, many of them by Margaret Hofmann. Many county records have been transcribed and published on a county by county basis by numerous individuals and organizations, although many counties remain virtually untouched by local history and genealogy publications. The library has actively acquired those records that have become available, including deeds, county court minutes, probate records, Court of Pleas and Quarter Sessions minutes, and vital records abstracted from local newspapers. The Mortality Schedules for the census years 1850-80 are also available on microfilm.

Bibliographies and Guides

Jeffrey J. Crow and Larry E. Tise. *Writing North Carolina History,* 1979. Very fine work on historiography.

Wallace R. Draughon and William Perry Johnson. *North Carolina Genealogical Reference.* 2nd ed., 1966.

Helen F. M. Leary and Maurice R. Stirewalt, eds. *North Carolina Research: Genealogy and Local History,* 1980. Excellent description of and guide to state and local records.

Hugh Talmage Lefler. *A Guide to the Study and Reading of North Carolina History.* 3rd ed., 1969. Good for beginners.

George K. Schweitzer. *North Carolina Genealogical Research,* 1984. Good.

George Stevenson. *North Carolina Local History, A Select Bibliography,* 1984. Very good.

Mary Lindsay Thornton. *A Bibliography of North Carolina, 1589-1956,* 1958.

Periodical and Serial Publications

The Carolina Genealogist. 52 nos., 1969-84.

North Carolina Booklet (North Carolina DAR). 23 vols., 1901-26.

The North Carolina Genealogical Society Journal, 1975 to date. One of the finest genealogical journals published in the United States.

North Carolina Genealogy. 21 vols., 1955-75.

North Carolina Historical and Genealogical Register. 3 vols., 1900-03.

North Carolina Historical Review, 1924 to date.

SOUTH CAROLINA

The South Carolina holdings at The Newberry Library, while not among the library's strongest state holdings, do contain all standard works and series, many early descriptive and settlement accounts, a number of local histories, and transcriptions and abstracts of records. When searching for early local records, researchers are reminded to check not only under the name of the county, but also under the judicial district, such as Ninety-six or Orangeburg. Although early district records were usually divided among the counties comprising that district, some printed sources have been published at the district level.

The Newberry Library collection contains many early description and travel accounts. A few of these are John Lawson's *A New Voyage to Carolina* (1709); John Archdale's *A New Description of that Fertile and Pleasant Province of Carolina* (1707); *A Relation of a Discovery Lately Made on the Coast of Florida* (1664) by William Hilton; and *A New and Accurate Account of the Provinces of South Carolina and Georgia...* (1732) attributed to James Oglethorpe.

A great many records and documents on South Carolina are in print, especially for the colonial period. In particular, the South Carolina Historical Society and the South Carolina Historical Commission have both been quite active in publishing original documents and records. The Newberry has five volumes of the *Collections of the South Carolina Historical Society* (1857-97), *The Colonial Records of South Carolina* (1951+), and *The State Records of South Carolina* (1956+), which include the journals of the Commons House of Assembly, journals of the Provincial Congress, journals of the Privy Council, journals of the House of Representatives, and documents and journals from the Civil War period.

Another important source for the Colonial period is *Records in the British Public Records Office Relating to South Carolina, 1663-1782.* This twelve-reel microfilm set contains handwritten transcripts from the Public Record Office. Selections from these transcripts were published in three volumes by the South Carolina Historical Commission (1928-31).

The Newberry also has a growing number of manuscript items on microfiche from the South Carolina Historical Society: Confederate military records including correspondence, orders, muster rolls, lists of officers; church registers, mostly for the Episcopal Church, and mostly in the form of transcripts; South Carolina land grants, 1735-52; and miscellaneous account books, plantation journals, letters, and diaries.

A good collection of genealogical source material is available. Early deed records for the state are indexed in *An Index to the Deeds of the Province and State of South Carolina, 1719-1785 and Charleston District, 1785-1800* (1977), compiled by Silas E. Lucas, Jr. Many colonial land records have been published, including *Warrants for Land in South Carolina, 1672-1711* (rev. ed., 1973), edited by A. S. Salley and R. N. Olsberg. In addition, many early deeds, county court minutes, and probate records have been published for individual counties. Early marriage bonds are found only infrequently in counties, but a number of individuals and societies, Brent Holcomb in particular, have been compiling vital records from South Carolina newspapers as a partial substitute for the county marriage records. Mortality Schedules for the census years 1850-80 are also part of the collection.

The Newberry has a good collection of local histories. Fifteen volumes of the annual *Charleston Year Book* are also available. The Newberry's volumes are from the years 1880-1900 and are a fine resource for social as well as local historians.

The French have been important in South Carolina since colonial times, and the library has a number of works on their presence in South Carolina, including the *Transactions of the Huguenot Society of South Carolina* (1889 +).

Bibliographies and Guides

Richard N. Cote. *Local and Family History in South Carolina: A Bibliography*, 1981. Good.

James H. Easterby. *Guide to the Study and Reading of South Carolina History*, 1950, reprinted with supplement 1975. Good selective bibliography.

Lewis P. Jones. *Books and Articles on South Carolina History: A List for Laymen*, 1970. Good for the beginner. Helpful annotations.

George K. Schweitzer. *South Carolina Genealogical Research*, 1985.

Robert J. Turnbull. *Bibliography of South Carolina, 1563-1950.* 6 vols., 1956-60. Books are arranged in chronological order.

Periodical and Serial Publications

The Carolina Genealogist. 52 nos., 1969-84.

Bulletin of the Chester County Genealogical Society, 1982 (vol. 5) to date.

The Proceedings and Papers of the Greenville County Historical Society, 1962 to date.

South Carolina Genealogical Register. 6 vols., 1963-68.

South Carolina Historical Magazine (formerly *South Carolina Historical and Genealogical Magazine*), 1900 to date.

South Carolina Magazine of Ancestral Research, 1973 to date.

TENNESSEE

Tennessee, one of the first areas of the Trans-Appalachian West to be settled, was an important center of migratory activity from the East (especially from the Carolinas and Virginia) into the South and Southwest. The Newberry has a good collection on the state including a number of rare volumes. A few of the more important and interesting ones are *A Concise Narrative of the Seminole Campaign. By an Officer Attached to the Expedition* (1819); *Recollections of the West* (1834) by Lewis Garrett; James Gray Smith's *A Brief Historical, Statistical and Descriptive Review of East Tennessee,...With Remarks to Emigrants. Accompanied with a Map & Lithographed Sketch of a Tennessee Farm, Mansion House, and Buildings* (1842), a promotional tract of the East Tennessee Land Company; and works by John Haywood, an early historian of Tennessee, including one of the earliest state histories, *The Civil and Political History of the State of Tennessee, From its Earliest Settlement Up to the Year 1796* (1823) and his rarest work, *The Christian Advocate* (1819), which has much on native Americans and archaeology.

The library's holdings of local histories are good, and very good for more recent works. These include volumes in the Tennessee County History Series (1979+) being published by Memphis State University Press, and all fifteen volumes of the Goodspeed Histories of Tennessee (1886-87), which cover eighty-two of the state's ninety-five counties. The library has a good collection on the State of Franklin (1785-88). Information on the State of Franklin can be located in the Card Catalogue under the subject heading "Franklin (State)." The holdings of genealogical source material are good and include many newspaper extracts of vital records, tax lists, and many transcripts of marriages. Most marriage transcripts are done on a county basis, with some covering larger geographical areas, for example, *35,000 Tennessee Marriage Records and Bonds, 1783-1870* (1981), edited by Silas E. Lucas, Jr. Also available are the Mortality Schedules for the census years 1850, 1860, and 1880.

The Lyman C. Draper Manuscripts contain much Tennessee material. See *Calendar of the Tennessee and King's Mountain Papers of the Draper Collection of Manuscripts* (1929), published by the State Historical Society of Wisconsin, and Chapter 10 of this book. Other important works are volume 4 of *The Territorial Papers of the United States,* which has many documents, letters, and petitions on early Tennessee, and Edythe J. Whitley's ten volumes of *Tennessee Genealogical Records* (1931-37). Researchers will also find a great deal on the Civil War in Tennessee.

Bibliographies and Guides
R. R. Allen. *Tennessee Books, A Preliminary Guide,* 1969.

Naomi Hailey. *A Guide to Genealogical Research in Tennessee,* 1979.

Laura Luttrell and Pollyanna Creekmore. "Writings on Tennessee Counties." *Tennessee Historical Quarterly* 2 (September and December 1943), 3 (March 1944).

George K. Schweitzer. *Tennessee Genealogical Research,* 1981. Good.

Sam B. Smith. *Tennessee History: A Bibliography,* 1974. Very good. Contains a lengthy bibliographic essay and a large, annotated, county history section.

Periodical and Serial Publications

American Historical Magazine and Tennessee Historical Society Quarterly. 9 vols., 1896-1904.

Coffee County Historical Society Quarterly, 1970 to date.

Publications of the East Tennessee Historical Society, 1929 to date. Contains the important series "Papers from the Spanish Archives Relating to Tennessee and the Old Southwest, 1783-1800."

Franklin County Historical Review, 1969 to date.

Publications of the Rutherford County Historical Society, 1976 (vol. 7) to date.

Tennessee Historical Magazine. 2 series, 1915-37.

Tennessee Historical Quarterly, 1942 to date.

Papers of the West Tennessee Historical Society, 1947 to date.

VIRGINIA

Virginia has had a long and colorful past, and much has been written on its state and local history. Still, doing local and family history research in Virginia does present some problems. Record keeping procedures differed from those found in New England, and that, along with the loss and destruction of many government records, often hampers researchers. Virginia has approximately twenty "Burned Record Counties," which have suffered substantial loss and destruction of records, many at the time of the Civil War.

Three works which index thousands of Virginians deserve mention. One of the most significant remains Earle G. Swem's *Virginia Historical Index* (1934-36), a name and subject index to seven important Virginia journals and historical sources. The Newberry has complete runs of all seven of the items. *The Biographical Dictionary of Early Virginia 1607-1660,* new edition (1982), a microfiche set published by the Association for the Preservation of Virginia Antiquities, includes nearly 30,000 people whose names appear in early Virginia records. Sixty-seven volumes of records were searched for this publication. Accompanying *The Biographical Dictionary* is *The Subject and Source Guide to Early Virginia, 1607-1660* (1982), edited by Ransom B. True. Patrick G. Wardell's *Timesaving Aid to Virginia/West Virginia Ancestors* (1985) is a listing of family names, along with references to printed works which contain information on the surname. Although Wardell duplicates some references readily available in other standard sources, he does include a number of important works which are inadequately indexed.

Despite the loss of many official records, a number of works have been published which transcribe or abstract the early records of Virginia. These include *The Records of the Virginia Company of London*, 4 volumes (1906-35); *Journals of the House of Burgesses*, 13 volumes (1905-15), covering 1619-1776; *Calendar of Virginia State Papers*, 11 volumes (1875-93), covering 1652-1869; *The Legislative Journals of the Council of Colonial Virginia*, 3 volumes (1918-19), covering 1680-1776; *The Executive Journals of the Council of Colonial Virginia*, 6 volumes (1925-66), covering 1680-1775; and *Journals of the Council of the State of Virginia*, 5 volumes (1931-82), covering 1776-1791, which is a continuation of the two previous series. Nell M. Nugent's *Cavaliers and Pioneers*, 3 volumes (1934-79), consists of abstracts of Virginia land patents and grants, including names of headrights to Virginia, making it an essential source on early immigration to and settlement in the Colony. The *Magazine of Virginia Genealogy* is now continuing Nugent's work beginning with the November, 1985 issue.

In addition to these transcriptions of early official documents, the Newberry also has a number of early and rare accounts of the discovery and settlement of Virginia. Among these are works by Capt. John Smith, *The Generall Historie of Virginia, New England, and the Summer Isles* (1624), and his 1612 map of Virginia; a very early account of Sir Walter Raleigh's 1585 expedition to Virginia in Theodore de Bry's *Admiranda Narratio, Fida Tamen, de Commodis et Incolarum Ritibus Virginiae* (1590); and *The History and Present State of Virginia* (1705) by Robert Beverley, the earliest printed history by a native Virginian. The library also has a great deal of material on colonial laws, including many early Acts of Assembly from 1744-63.

The Newberry Library has a good collection of printed local histories and genealogical source material. A large amount of material will be found in *Virginia Colonial Abstracts*, 40 volumes in 2 series (1937-62), series I by Beverley Fleet and series II by Lindsay O. Duvall. The Lyman C. Draper Manuscripts are available at the Newberry and contain a great deal on western Virginia and West Virginia. See Mabel C. Weaks' *The Preston and Virginia Papers of the Draper Collection of Manuscripts* (1915) and Chapter 10 of this guide. Marriage records have been published for many counties, as have increasing numbers of probate and court records. Because of Virginia's rather late start in keeping vital records, a number of indexes have appeared to marriages, obituaries, and other genealogical data from newspapers. Church records are important sources, and the Newberry has much on the Protestant Episcopal Church, which prior to 1786 was the established church of Virginia. This material includes church histories, cemetery transcriptions, descriptions of parish boundary lines, and all of the handful of published parish registers and vestry books. A number of early Virginia censuses are missing, and in several cases tax lists, which begin for all Virginia counties in 1782, have been published as substitutes. The Mortality Schedules for the census years 1850-80 are also part of the library's holdings.

Two other series which contain much of interest to local and family historians are *Collections of the Virginia Historical Society,* 12 volumes (1833-92), and the Virginia Historical Society's Documents Series (1961+). Virginia was a major battlefield in both the Revolutionary War and the Civil War, and not surprisingly, there is a great deal of material on military engagements and military affairs in the state.

Bibliographies and Guides

Stuart E. Brown, Jr. *Virginia Genealogies.* 2 vols., 1967-80. Good list of printed books and pamphlets.

Lester J. Cappon. *Bibliography of Virginia History Since 1865,* 1930. Outstanding work, although somewhat out of date. Brief annotations are very helpful.

Robert Y. Clay. *Virginia Genealogical Resources,* 1980. Excellent guide, of value to local historians as well as genealogists.

"Guide to the Counties of Virginia." A continuing series, proceeding alphabetically through the counties, begun in volume 3 (1959) of *The Virginia Genealogist.*

George K. Schweitzer. *Virginia Genealogical Research,* 1982.

Robert A. Stewart. *Index to Printed Virginia Genealogies,* 1930.

Virginia State Library. *Virginia Local History, A Bibliography,* 1971. Primarily books, along with a few periodical articles.

Virginia State Library. *Virginiana in the Printed Book Collections of the Virginia State Library,* 1975.

Periodical and Serial Publications

Magazine of Albemarle County History, 1940 to date.

Augusta Historical Bulletin, 1965 to date.

The Bulletin of the Fluvanna County Historical Society, 1965 to date.

Magazine of Virginia Genealogy (formerly the *Virginia Genealogical Society Quarterly*), 1961 to date.

Northern Neck Historical Magazine, 1951 to date.

Journal of the Roanoke Valley Historical Society. 11 vols., 1964-80.

Proceedings of the Rockbridge Historical Society, 1939 to date.

The Rockingham Recorder, 1945 to date.

The Southside Virginian, 1982 to date.

Tyler's Quarterly Historical and Genealogical Magazine. 34 vols., 1919-52.

The Virginia Genealogist, 1957 to date.

The Virginia Magazine of History and Biography, 1894 to date.

Virginia Historical Register. 6 vols., 1848-53.

William and Mary College Quarterly, 1892 to date. The premier journal on colonial North America.

WEST VIRGINIA

West Virginia separated from its parent state during the Civil War, and researchers must remember that many references to families, individuals, and locations in West Virginia are found in Virginia sources. Please read the preceding chapter on Virginia for additional information on pre-statehood West Virginia.

The Newberry's holdings of local histories are good, although there are few transcriptions of genealogical source material such as vital records, deeds, probates, or church records. This is primarily because until recent years few publications of this type had appeared; however, West Virginia is one of the few states that has much of its 1880 census transcribed and indexed. The *1880 Census of West Virginia* (1979+), compiled by William A. Marsh, is not a state-wide index, but is being done on a county-by-county basis. The counties are not being published in alphabetical order. West Virginia lacks a multi-volume "state papers" or "collections of the state historical society" series. For the twentieth century, the library does have twenty-six volumes of the *West Virginia Blue Book* published between 1926 and 1957, which provide good information on government officials and agencies.

Periodicals are often overlooked by local and family historians, partly because it is often difficult to determine readily the contents of various journals and magazines. West Virginia researchers are fortunate to have Robert F. Munn's *Index to West Virginiana* (1960), which indexes twelve periodicals, excluding *West Virginia History*. Five of these periodicals are found at the Newberry.

Bibliographies and Guides
Innis C. Davis. *A Bibliography of West Virginia,* 1939. Not as useful as

Shetler or Forbes, but does include official state documents.

Harold M. Forbes. *West Virginia History: A Bibliography and Guide to Research,* 1981. Good, but not annotated. Basically an update of Shetler.

Charles Shetler. *Guide to the Study of West Virginia History*, 1960.

Periodical and Serial Publications

Magazine of the Jefferson County Historical Society, 1935 to date (some early issues are missing).

Kith and Kin of Boone County, 1977 to date.

Upper Ohio Valley Historical Review, 1977 (vol. 7) to date.

West Virginia Echoer, 1967 to date.

West Virginia Historical Magazine Quarterly. 5 vols., 1901-05.

West Virginia History, 1939 to date.

CHAPTER 14

THE MIDWEST

The states of the Midwest, which form the geographical heart of the United States, have also served as a magnet, attracting settlers from the East, the South and from Europe. The Newberry's midwestern holdings are the strongest for any region in the U. S. Those holdings for Ohio, Indiana, Illinois, and Iowa are particularly rich.

An excellent collection of description and travel accounts will be found. These range from such early accounts as Father Louis Hennepin's *Description de la Louisiane* (1683) and Baron de Lahontan's *New Voyages to North America* (1703) to nineteenth-century travellers' and emigrants' guides such as Randolph B. Marcy's *Prairie Traveler* (1859), James Hall's *Letters From the West; Containing Sketches of Scenery, Manners, and Customs;...* (1828), and Samuel R. Brown's *The Western Gazetteer; or, Emigrants' Directory, Containing a Geographical Description of the Western States and Territories...* (1817).

Solon J. Buck's *Travel and Description 1765-1865. Together With a List of County Histories, Atlases, and Biographical Collections and a List of Territorial and State Laws* (Collections of the Illinois State Historical Library, vol. 9, 1914) is a fine bibliography of description and travel accounts. Although it is devoted to Illinois, most of the accounts also cover other parts of the Midwest. The collection is very strong for works on frontier and pioneer life, directories, and personal reminiscences. Local history holdings are very good to excellent, as are the holdings of genealogical source material and census schedules.

Periodical and Serial Publications

Inland Seas, 1945 to date.

The Old Northwest, 1975 to date.

The Old Northwest Genealogical Quarterly. 15 vols., 1898-1912.

Upper Midwest History, 1981 to date.

ILLINOIS

It will come as no surprise to learn that the Newberry's Illinois holdings are among the library's strongest. The breadth, depth, and size of the collection makes the Newberry one of the most important institutions for the study of Illinois local and family history.

Excellent material is available on description and travel accounts, personal reminiscences, frontier and pioneer life, gazetteers, directories, state and federal census schedules, local histories, genealogical source material, and bibliographies and research guides. There is also very good material on the Mormons in Illinois.

Several state-wide sources are useful to researchers. *Illinois Public Domain Land Sale Records,* from the Illinois State Archives, is one important source on early Illinois and its people. Over one-half million names appear in these records, which include lands sold by the ten federal land district offices in Illinois, lands sold by the Illinois Central Railroad, and certain school, canal, and internal improvements lands sold by the state. The Land Sale Records are in three parts--a state-wide alphabetical listing by name of purchaser, a county-by-county listing arranged alphabetically by purchaser, and a geographical listing arranged by section, township, and range. An additional source complementing the Land Sale Records is a microfilm of the original General Land Office plats for the entire state, as well as surveyors' field notes.

Now available on microfiche is a compilation of pre-1900 Illinois marriage records, produced through the joint efforts of the Illinois State Genealogical Society and the Illinois State Archives. The first installment contains approximately 80,000 marriages. The "Index to Compiled Service Records of Volunteer Union Soldiers who Served in Organizations from the State of Illinois" is another important state-wide source. This is the index to the National Archives records; the library does not have the service records themselves. *Honor Roll, State of Illinois,* compiled by the Illinois Veterans' Commission, is another source on military service and veterans, although not one hundred percent complete. This multi-volume set attempts to record all veterans buried in Illinois cemeteries prior to July 1, 1955. An earlier, two-volume Illinois *Roll of Honor* was published in 1929.

Several serial publications, often overlooked by researchers, contain much important local and family history information. The Collections of the Illinois State Historical Library (1903-58), has early census returns, records of the Black Hawk War, and much information on the French in Illinois. Another important series is the *Fergus Historical Series,* 35 numbers (1876-1914). While this is generally considered a Chicago resource, it does contain some early records and history of Illinois, and biographical sketches and reminiscences of early settlers.

The collection of Illinois local histories is excellent. The library also has an every-name index to at least one county history for each of Illinois' 102 counties. Useful information on early Illinoisans is found in *The Territorial Papers of the United States,* volumes 16 and 17 on Illinois Territory, and volume 7 on Indiana Territory. Names of many early settlers appear on petitions and letters recorded in *The Territorial Papers.* All pre-1860 directories for the state are available, as well as a great many for later years, both from rural areas and cities and towns. The library holds an excellent collection of genealogical source material, including complete runs of all Illinois genealogical society quarterlies (but not newsletters), and virtually all society publications. The *Blue Books* and *Grandparent Files* compiled by Illinois DAR chapters are another important source of genealogical information. The *Blue Books* contain family histories, cemetery records, Bible records, marriages, vital records, and much more. Each year the Illinois DAR donates copies of its *Blue Books* to the Newberry. The collection of *Blue Books,* which began in the 1930s, now numbers several hundred volumes.

The Newberry holds all extant Illinois state and federal census schedules, including the federal mortality, agricultural, and manufacturing schedules for the census years 1850-80. The Illinois state census is a head-of-household census only. For further information on the census holdings, indexes, and other finding aids, see Chapter 13.

There is a large body of material on state politics, government, and constitutional conventions. It includes the *Illinois Blue Book* (not to be confused with the DAR *Blue Book*) for 1900, 1903-07, and 1917/18-1961/62, plus several earlier legislative manuals beginning with 1871. The Newberry has the *Journal of the Illinois General Assembly, House of Representatives,* 9th-51st sessions (1835-1919), and *Journal of the Senate,* 5th-51st sessions (1826-1919), plus reports of the General Assembly, messages of governors, and some early statutes.

Bibliographies and Guides

Solon Justus Buck. *Travel and Description, 1765-1865: Together with a List of County Histories, Atlases, and Biographical Collections and a List of Territorial and State Laws.* Collections of The Illinois State Historical Library, vol. IX, 1914. Despite its age, still a very important resource.

Lowell Volkel and Marjorie Smith. *How to Research a Family with Illinois Roots,* 1977.

Joseph C. Wolf. *A Reference Guide for Genealogical and Historical Research in Illinois,* 1963. Good. Includes county bibliographies.

Contemporary Newspapers and Journals

Illinois Monthly Magazine (also called *The Western Monthly Magazine*), 1831-37.

Oquawka Spectator, February-December 1848 and February-December 1851.

Republican and Gazette (Sterling), July 1856-April 1862.

Times and Seasons (Nauvoo), 1839-46. Mormon publication.

Periodical and Serial Publications

Illinois Historical Journal (formerly *Journal of the Illinois State Historical Society*), 1908 to date.

Illinois Magazine (formerly *Outdoor Illinois*), 1965 (vol. 4) to date.

Illinois State Genealogical Society Quarterly, 1969 to date.

Collections of the Illinois State Historical Library. 33 vols., 1903-58.

Transactions of the Illinois State Historical Society, 1899 to date.

Mennonite Heritage (Illinois Mennonite Historical and Genealogical Society), 1974 to date.

Mid-America (Illinois Catholic Historical Society). 50 vols., 1918-68. Not limited to Illinois.

Polish Genealogical Society Newsletter, 1979 to date.

Journal of the St. Clair County Historical Society, 1965 to date.

Search (Jewish Genealogical Society of Illinois), 1981 to date.

Western Illinois Regional Studies, 1978 to date.

The Newberry also has all Illinois Genealogical Society quarterlies.

CHICAGO AND SURROUNDING COUNTIES

All too often researchers wrongly assume that since The Newberry Library is in Chicago, it has "everything" one needs to consult on Chicago area local history and genealogy. While the Newberry is certainly one of the primary institutions for Chicago local history and genealogy, the library does not have everything needed by researchers, and in certain areas, other institutions have better, or more complete holdings. This section will attempt to acquaint researchers with some of the major available sources. Many of these are covered in greater detail in other parts of this guide, and researchers are urged to refer to the appropriate chapters.

In general the Newberry does not collect United States history for the post-World War I period, although for Chicago the collecting period does extend into the 1920s and 1930s. The library has a good collection of the standard histories and monographs, although it is not the largest or most comprehensive collection in the city. The collection is strong for church histories and anniversary publications, works on Chicago suburbs, and certain ethnic groups in Chicago (primarily Germans, Irish, and Poles). There is limited material on Chicago neighborhoods. The library has some, but not all, Chicago newspapers, although the collection is very good for German language newspapers. The Newberry has no suburban newspapers. For further information see Chapter 2.

The Newberry does have a complete set of Chicago city directories, which appeared from 1839-1928/29. There are also three directories arranged by *address only* for 1952, 1953, and 1955. Some suburban directories, including ones for Oak Park, Evanston, and Town of Lake (now part of Chicago), are also available. The library has Chicago alphabetical telephone books from 1914-1960, 1970-1980. Some classified and suburban telephone directories are found as well. Many of the telephone books are extremely fragile and must be handled with great care.

Finding aids and/or indexes are available to assist those doing census searches in the city. Among these is a microfilm set from the Illinois State Archives, entitled "Name Index to Early Illinois Records: Index to 1860 Census of Chicago and Cook County." Despite the title, this set contains only the 1860 census index, not other early Illinois records. See Chapter 3 for further information. The Newberry's Chicago and Cook County Biography and Industry File is an important and ever-growing source of biographical information. Researchers may wish to consult Chapter 9, "Department of Special Collections," for Modern Manuscript holdings relating to Chicago.

In addition to all the printed works on churches, synagogues, and religious groups in Chicago and surrounding counties, the library also has microfilms of original church records of several area congregations:

First Presbyterian Church of Wheaton (formerly the First Church of Christ), 1866-1980;

St. John United Church of Christ, Naperville (formerly Evangelical Lutheran Church of St. John the Evangelist), 1860-1942;

Evangelical Lutheran Church of St. Luke, Chicago, 1884-1975;

St. James Evangelical Lutheran Church, Chicago, 1870-1951.

The library is also due to receive the microfilmed parish registers of all parishes of the Roman Catholic Archdiocese of Chicago founded prior to 1915. These microfilms will come to the library through the cooperative efforts of the Archdiocese, the Genealogical Society of Utah and the Council of Northeastern Illinois Genealogical Societies. The Newberry has been designated as the depository for the non-official records filmed by the Genealogical Society of Utah in the Chicago area. These microfilms are beginning to arrive at the Newberry and presently consist of church records from several North Shore communities. Additional microfilms may include cemetery records, funeral home records, and other miscellaneous sources.

The Newberry does not have the official Cook County birth, death, marriage, probate, or land records. Only a few area cemeteries have been transcribed, and they are all found at the library. Several have appeared in local genealogical society periodicals and publications. Some early Chicago vital statistics are found in Sam Fink's "Marriages and Deaths, Chicago Newspapers, 1834-1889." Ten Chicago newspapers were consulted in compiling this manuscript.

Bibliographies and Guides

Frank Jewell. *Annotated Bibliography of Chicago History,* 1979. Highly selective.

Margaret O'Hara. *Finding Your Chicago Ancestor,* 1982.

Loretto Dennis Szucs. *Chicago and Cook County Sources: A Genealogical and Historical Guide,* 1986. Very important. The essential source for Chicago researchers.

Periodical and Serial Publications

The Chicago Genealogist, 1969 to date.

Chicago History, 1945 to date.

Fergus Historical Series. 35 nos., 1876-1914. Very good source, not limited to Chicago. Contains biographical sketches of early settlers, reminiscences of early Chicago, papers, addresses, and lectures.

Hyde Park History, 1980 to date.

Lake County Genealogical Society Quarterly, 1980 to date.

Where the Trails Cross (South Suburban Genealogical and Historical Society), 1970 to date.

Will-Grundy Counties Genealogical Society Quarterly, 1982 to date.

INDIANA

Indiana, which sits at the center of the Midwest, has been a major throughway and stopping-off point of the westward migration, and its population is very representative of the southern, eastern, and European influxes that came together in the Midwest. The Newberry's Indiana holdings are excellent--they are among the library's strongest state collections. The collection is excellent for description and travel accounts, directories, gazetteers, genealogical source material, works on frontier and pioneer life, and local histories.

There are voluminous amounts of genealogical source material, probably the largest collection in the library. Researchers will find extensive holdings of transcripts, indexes and abstracts of vital records, probates, deeds, marriages, cemetery records, naturalizations, church records, county commissioners' records, and more. For most counties, records of births, deaths, and marriages to 1920 are available, compiled under the auspices of the Works Progress Administration (WPA). Each county also has, or will soon have, a volume entitled *Index of Names of Persons and Firms.* These volumes index a number of the county histories and atlases published on each county. The WPA compiled volumes for each county alphabetically through Madison County; the Family History Section of the Indiana Historical Society is completing the remaining counties. The library also has an index to the Indiana Mortality Schedules for the census years 1850-80, plus a great deal on land records. These include abstracts and indexes for several of the federal land offices, Clark's grant, the Vincennes donation lands, and early deed records for many counties.

Other important sources include *The Territorial Papers of the United States,* volumes 7 and 8; all pre-1860 directories on microfiche; *Indiana Source Book,* 3 volumes (1977-82), by Willard Heiss and Dorothy Riker, which contains extracts from *The Hoosier Genealogist*; and *Indiana Biographical Index* (1983) by Genealogical Indexing Associates. This last item is an index to biographical sketches taken from 537 works, including many county histories.

Serial publications by several Indiana historical organizations are important sources. The Newberry has Indiana Historical Collections (1916+), by the Indiana Historical Bureau, which includes works on local history, biographies, journals of the Territorial General Assembly, several volumes on politics and political figures, description and travel accounts, and *Indiana World War Records, Gold Star Honor Roll* (1921), an album of those who died in World War I. Also available is *Yearbook of the Society of Indiana Pioneers* (1921+); *Indiana Historical Society Publications* (1897+), which is good for diaries and journals, frontier and pioneer life, reminiscences, and local histories; and *Steel Shavings* (1975+) by Indiana University Northwest in Gary.

Bibliographies and Guides

Carolynne L. (Wendel) Miller. *Indiana Sources For Genealogical Research in the Indiana State Library,* 1984. Very good. Includes sources from the State Library Genealogy Division only, so few local histories are included.

Carolynne L. Wendel. *Aids for Genealogical Searching in Indiana,* 1962 (a 1970 revised edition has been published). Very useful bibliographies.

Malinda E. E. Newhard. *A Guide to Genealogical Records in Indiana.* 2nd ed., 1981. Good.

Periodical and Serial Publications

Family Fare (Allen County Public Library). Volumes 1-14, 18; 1961-78.

Genealogy. 100 numbers, 1973-86. Not limited to Indiana. One of the country's finest genealogical journals.

The Hoosier Genealogist, 1961 to date.

Hoosier Journal of Ancestry, 1969 to date.

Indiana History Bulletin. 46 vols., 1923-69.

Indiana Magazine of History, 1905 to date.

Northwest Trail Tracer (Knox County), 1980 to date.

Old Fort News (Fort Wayne), 1967 (vol. 30) to date.

South Bend Area Genealogical Society Quarterly, 1976 to date.

Southern Indiana Genealogical Society Quarterly, 1980 to date.

IOWA

The Iowa holdings of The Newberry Library are surpassed in size, scope, and quality only by the library's Illinois collection. The collection is excellent for description and travel accounts, frontier and pioneer life, gazetteers, emigrant guides, material on land companies, directories, and genealogical source material. For most counties at least some transcripts of marriages, vital records, cemetery listings, or other genealogical source materials are available. The holdings of local histories are also excellent, both for nineteenth-century works and more recent publications. Two of the earliest Iowa local histories, both at the Newberry, are H. B. Turrill's *Historical Reminiscences of the City of Des Moines, Together with a Full Description of the City and County,...* (1857) and *Muscatine City Directory and Advertiser, For 1856: Containing a History of the City and County* (1856).

A number of very rare Iowa books and manuscripts are at the Newberry, most of them part of the Graff Collection. Everett D. Graff was born in Clarinda, Iowa and retained an interest in his native state. Some examples from the Graff Collection are the very interesting autograph manuscripts of William Hillhouse entitled "Incidents and Experiences" and "In Iowa," covering the years 1840-44. Hillhouse was an Indian trader in Iowa. Another manuscript document is the Articles of Agreement by which the city of Davenport was established in 1836.

Researchers will also find a great many publications, annuals and reunion reports from old settlers' societies and pioneer associations in the state; quite a bit on Keokuk; the *Iowa Territorial Gazette and Burlington Advertiser,* July 1837-June 1840, on microfilm; the *Page County Herald,* June 1859-May 1862; the *Council Bluffs Bugle,* November 1853-October 1856; all pre-1860 Iowa directories on microfiche; part of the

1915 Iowa State Census; some Quaker Monthly Meeting records taken from William Wade Hinshaw's unpublished transcripts at Swarthmore College; the Johnson County (Iowa City) Probate Court records, 1840-1903, on microfilm; and a very large collection of Iowa DAR records, including some grandparent forms, family histories, transcripts of records, and other "Blue Book" contributions, as well as 8 volumes of *Iowa Pioneers: Their Ancestors and Descendants,* (1969-76) and 6 volumes of *Iowa Pioneer Families* (n.d.). Most publications of the Iowa State Historical Society are also part of the Newberry holdings.

Bibliographies and Guides

Luella E. Cook. "Histories of Iowa Counties," *Iowa Journal of History and Politics* 36 (1938): 115-51. Still useful for early works.

Charles Morford. *Biographical Index to the County Histories of Iowa* (1979). Indexes approximately 44,000 biographies taken from 130 county histories.

Frank Luther Mott. *Literature of Pioneer Life in Iowa* (1923). Very good.

William J. Petersen. *Iowa History Reference Guide* (1952). Includes books and articles; no annotations.

Elsie L. Sopp. *Personal Name Index to the 1856 City Directories of Iowa* (1980). Includes 15,000 names from 7 Iowa counties and 3 Illinois cities.

Periodical and Serial Publications

Annals of Iowa, 1863 to date.

Blackhawk Genealogical Society Quarterly (Quad Cities), 1974 to date.

Hawkeye Heritage (Iowa Genealogical Society), 1966 to date.

The Iowa Historical Record, 18 vols., 1885-1902. Continued as *Iowa Journal of History and Politics,* 59 vols., 1903-61.

The Palimpsest (State Historical Society of Iowa), 1920 to date.

Taylor County, Iowa Genealogical Group, 1974 to date.

MICHIGAN

The Newberry Library's Michigan holdings, although not among the strongest for the midwestern states, still contain much of interest to local and family historians and are quite strong for certain topics. The collection is very strong on the French influence in Michigan, which was the center of French activity in the Great Lakes area. This includes much material on Detroit and the Mackinac Region before 1800. The library also has very good material on description and travel accounts, reminiscences, frontier and pioneer life, and emigrant guides. The holdings on frontier and pioneer life include such important titles as William Nowlin's *The Bark Covered House* (1876), and Catherine Stewart's *New Homes in the West* (1843).

Researchers will also find good material on boundary disputes, James Jesse Strang and the Mormon settlement on Beaver Island, and the Lake Superior region and the Upper Peninsula. Works on the Upper Peninsula are found in the Card Catalogue under the subject heading "Michigan, Northern Peninsula," with a few works also listed under "Michigan, Upper Peninsula." The Beaver Island material includes the significant Strang work, *The Book of the Law of the Lord...* in both the 1851 preliminary edition and the 1856 edition. The local history holdings are good. Michigan has not produced as much genealogical source material as other midwestern states. Thus the Newberry holdings are rather small, although good when referenced with what has appeared in print.

One of the most important works on Michigan is *Michigan Pioneer and Historical Collections,* 40 volumes (1876-1929). This series includes biographies, reminiscences, local historical accounts, Indian captivity narratives, and much more. Other useful sources are *The Territorial Papers of the United States,* volumes 10 to 12; Occasional Papers from the Mid-Michigan Genealogical Society (1968+); and *Michigan Official Directory and Legislative Manual,* 41 volumes (1881-1964), which contains biographies of state legislators and information on government, state institutions, railroads, and the press. The library also has partial runs of two newspapers: *Detroit Gazette* (1817-30); and *Detroit Free Press* (1861-79, incomplete).

Bibliographies and Guides

Alloa C. Anderson and Polly Bender. *Genealogy in Michigan, What, When, Where.* 2nd ed., 1978.

Albert Harry Greenly. *A Selective Bibliography of Important Books, Pamphlets and Broadsides Relating to Michigan History,* 1958. Very good, but only covers about 125 important books.

Michigan Historical Collections, University of Michigan. *Bibliography of Michigan County Histories,* 1951. Not annotated.

Michigan Magazine Index, 1965-78. Indexes over 150 periodicals. Not limited to historical or genealogical material.

Maud Quigley. *Index to Michigan Research Found in Genealogical Periodicals,* 1979. Good. Indexes eighty-one genealogical periodicals from many states.

Floyd Benjamin Streeter. *Michigan Bibliography,* 1921. Includes books, maps, manuscripts and pamphlets through July 1917. Still useful.

Periodical and Serial Publications

Detroit Society for Genealogical Research Magazine, 1937 to date.

The Eaglet (Polish Genealogical Society of Michigan), 1981 to date.

Family Trails (Michigan Department of Education, Bureau of Library Services), 1967 to date.

Heir-Lines (North Oakland Genealogical Society), 1978 to date.

Kalamazoo Valley Family Newsletter. 8 vols., 1971-78.

Michigan Heritage. 14 vols., 1959-73.

Michigan Historical Review (Formerly *Great Lakes Review*), 1974 to date.

Michigan History, 1917 to date.

Michigan Jewish History, 1960 to date.

Timbertown Log (Saginaw Genealogical Society), 1972 to date.

MINNESOTA

Minnesota, which brings to mind images of Scandinavians, lakes, and flour mills, became a state in 1858, although it was not until the 1880s, when homesteaders poured into the state, that settlement began in earnest. The Newberry Library has a fair collection of Minnesota material. The holdings are good for travel and description accounts, works on frontier and pioneer life, emigrant guides, promotional/boosterism literature, publications of the Minnesota Historical Society, the Scandinavians in Minnesota, the U. S. Army in the state, and contact with the Indians. The local history holdings are fair, somewhat better for book-length county and regional histories than for pamphlet histories. Much Minnesota local history has appeared in pamphlet form, and only a small number of these are found at the library. Among the holdings are two of the earliest Minnesota local histories: W. H. Mitchell's *Dakota County. Its Past and Present...* (1868) and the first history of Minnesota's first settlement, W. H. Mitchell's and J. H. Stevens's *Geographical and Statistical History of the County of Hennepin,...* (1869). A small amount of genealogical source material is available.

A number of gazetteers, manuals, and directories may be of help to researchers. The library has the *Minnesota State Gazetteer* (some volumes also include the Dakotas and Montana) for 1880/81, 1882/83, 1888/89, 1906/07, 1912/13, 1920/21, and 1926. This is a state-wide business directory, divided into two parts: a list of businesses in each town and a state-wide list by type of business. Also available are city directories for Moorhead, Minnesota, and Fargo, North Dakota, for 1881-1927 on microfiche; Minneapolis directories for 1887-1927; and St. Paul directories for 1863-1869/70, 1885-1930. *Minnesota Year Book* (1851, 1852, 1853), and *The Legislative Manual of the State of Minnesota* (1877, 1893, 1899-1901, 1905, and 1921-1957/58) contain biographical sketches of government officials and legislators, election returns, and information on state institutions, offices, and commissions.

The Newberry has on microfilm from the Minnesota Historical Society the papers of two important Minnesotans: Henry Hastings Sibley, a fur trader, civic leader, and Minnesota's first state governor; and Lawrence Taliaferro, Indian Agent at Fort Snelling.

Bibliographies and Guides

Theodore C. Blegen. *Minnesota, Its History and Its People: A Study Outline with Topics and References,* 1937. Intended for classroom use. Dated but still somewhat useful.

Michael Brook. *Reference Guide to Minnesota History; A Subject Bibliography,* 1974, plus 1983 supplement. Very good. Books, articles and pamphlets are arranged under thirty-two subject headings.

Arthur L. Finnell. *Minnesota Genealogical Periodical Index: A County Guide,* 1980. Indexes seven periodicals and newsletters. The Newberry has only one of the seven--*Minnesota Genealogist.*

Wiley R. Pope. *Tracing Your Ancestors in Minnesota.* 2 volumes, 1978-81. Volume 1 covers Minnesota in general, volume 2 covers South Central Minnesota. Has useful county bibliographies.

Robert B. Porter. *How to Trace Your Minnesota Ancestors,* 1985.

Warren Upham and Rose B. Dunlap. *Minnesota Biographies, 1655-1912.* Minnesota Historical Society Collections, vol. 14, 1912. Contains sketches of about 9,000 individuals taken from 250 sources, including many local histories.

Periodical and Serial Publications

Minnesota Genealogical Journal, 1984 to date.

Minnesota Genealogist, 1970 to date.

Minnesota Historical Society Collections. 17 vols., 1872-1920.

Minnesota History, 1915 to date.

Ramsey County History, 1964 to date.

Red River Valley Historian. Volumes 2-12, 1968-78.

MISSOURI

Missouri, settled from both the North and the South, exhibits characteristics of each region. Local and family historians will find a good Missouri collection at The Newberry Library. Holdings are very good for description and travel accounts; guides and gazetteers; the Mormons in Missouri; and published material on the French and Spanish colonial periods. Local history holdings are good and include the Goodspeed histories of Missouri. There is also good information on Missouri outlaws, the Civil War in the state, and the St. Louis Exposition of 1904.

In recent years there has been an outpouring of genealogical works, and the library has a good collection of genealogical source material. Many marriage records have been published, as well as cemetery transcriptions, obituary listings, newspaper abstracts, and land claims and grants. The library has several major genealogical compilations including *Missouri Miscellany,* 17 volumes (1976-84) by Audrey L. Woodruff; *Missouri Pioneers,* 30 volumes (1967-76) by Woodruff and Nadine Hodges; and the numerous works of Elizabeth P. Ellsberry.

Several nineteenth century Missouri periodicals and newspapers are part of the collection. They include *St. Louis Reveille* (May 1844-October 1850); *Western Journal of Commerce* (Kansas City, October 1857-June 1866); *Missouri Gazette* (St. Louis, July 1808-December 1818); and *The Western Journal and Civilian, Devoted to Agriculture, Manufactures, Mechanic Arts, Internal Improvement, Commerce, Public Policy, and Polite Literature...* (St. Louis, January 1848-March 1856).

Several other sources also deserve mention: volumes 13-15 of *The Territorial Papers of the United States* are good for territorial documents, letters, and petitions; the six-volume *Collections of the Missouri Historical Society* (1880-1929), which contain diaries and journals, biographies, family genealogies, local histories, reminiscences, and memoirs (often lengthy) of deceased members; Frances Terry Ingmire's *Citizens of Missouri Territory,* 3 volumes (1984); and Russell L. Gerlach's *Immigrants in the Ozarks: A Study in Ethnic Geography* (1976), which provides good background material on the Ozark counties and a helpful account of settlement patterns of ethnic groups.

Bibliographies and Guides

Robert E. Parkin. *Parkin's Guide to Tracing Your Family Tree in Missouri,* 1979. Very good bibliographies and some helpful maps.

Paul O. Selby. *A Bibliography of Missouri County Histories and Atlases,* 1966. Good, but not annotated.

Selwyn K. Troen. *A Guide to Resources on the History of Saint Louis,* 1971. Very good, includes books, articles, and dissertations.

Jacqueline Hogan Williams and Betty Harvey Williams. *Resources for Genealogical Research in Missouri,* 1969.

Periodical and Serial Publications

Bulletin of the Missouri Historical Society. 36 vols., 1944-80. Superseded by *Gateway Heritage,* 1980 to date.

Glimpses of the Past (Missouri Historical Society). 10 vols., 1933-43.

Missouri Historical Review, 1906 to date.

Missouri State Genealogical Association Journal, 1981 to date.

Pioneer Times (Mid-Missouri Genealogical Society), 1978 (vol. 2) to date.

St. Louis Genealogical Society Quarterly, 1968 to date.

Westport Historical Quarterly. 10 vols., 1965-75.

OHIO

Ohio, the first area of the Northwest Territory to gain statehood has, because of its geographical position, served as a corridor funneling settlers from the east to the west along Lake Erie, down the Ohio River, and across the state on various roads, railways, and canals. The Ohio holdings of The Newberry Library rank among the best and largest of the state holdings. The collection is very good to excellent for description and travel accounts, works on frontier and pioneer life, boundary disputes, land records, census records, and works on such land companies as the Scioto Land Company and the Ohio Company.

The holdings of local histories are excellent, as are the holdings of genealogical source material. The collection of genealogical source material is one of the largest in the library and includes compilations and abstracts of vital records, marriages, cemeteries, probate records, deeds, tax lists, newspaper abstracts, church records, and much more. This is in part due to the large number of publications produced by local chapters of the Ohio Genealogical Society and many individuals, all of which the Newberry has actively collected. Two important state-wide works are Carol Willsey Bell's *Ohio Wills and Estates to 1850: An Index* (1981) and *Ohio Cemeteries* (1978) by the Ohio Genealogical Society. The latter lists cemeteries only, not all burials.

The library has extensive material on Ohio land records and land grants. *Ohio Land Grant Records 1788-1820,* on seven reels of microfilm, covers the federal land offices at Chillicothe, Cincinnati, Steubenville, and Zanesville. This set is incompletely indexed in Mayburt Stephenson Riegel's *Early Ohioans Residences from the Land Grant Records* (1976). The early Steubenville land office records were published by Carol Willsey Bell, *Ohio Lands: Steubenville Land Office, 1800-1820* (1983), and Chris McHenry has published *Symmes Purchase Records...* (1979). Clifford Neal Smith's *Federal Land Series,* 4 volumes (1972-82) covers much of Ohio. The library also has transcripts of deed records for many counties and monographs on the land issue.

Some other important sources include the Mortality Schedules for the census years 1850, 1860, and 1880, all pre-1860 directories on microfiche, many post-1860 directories, and two Cincinnati newspapers: *Cincinnati Daily Commercial* (July 1861-December 1886, incomplete), and *Charles Cist's Weekly Advertiser* (February 1844-April 1853). Two Works Progress Administration compilations are available: *Annals of Cleveland, 1818-1935*, a digest and index from Cleveland newspapers, and *Annals of Cleveland, Court Records Series*, which consists of abstracts and indexes of court records from 1837-75.

Bibliographies and Guides

Carol Willsey Bell. *Ohio Genealogical Guide*. 3rd ed., 1984. Excellent source.

_____. *Ohio Genealogical Periodical Index: A County Guide*. 3rd ed., 1981. A 4th edition (1983) is now available. Indexes seventy-five publications.

Petta Khouw and Genealogy Staff of The State Library of Ohio. *County by County in Ohio Genealogy*, 1978. Good bibliographies.

Peter Gibson Thomson. *A Bibliography of the State of Ohio...*, 1880, repr. 1966. Still useful.

Periodical and Serial Publications

The Firelands Pioneer. 3 ser., 1858-1937, 1980 to date.

Gateway to the West. 11 vols., 1967-78.

The Quarterly Publication of the Historical and Philosophical Society of Ohio. 18 vols., 1906-23.

Northwest Ohio Quarterly (Maumee Valley Historical Society), 1929 to date.

Ohio Genealogical Helper, 1975 to date.

The Ohio Genealogical Quarterly. 8 vols., 1937-44.

Ohio Genealogical Society Report, 1961 to date.

Ohio Historical Collections. 11 vols., 1930-44.

Ohio History (formerly *Ohio Archaeological and Historical Quarterly* and *Ohio Historical Quarterly*), 1887 to date.

Ohio Records and Pioneer Families (Ohio Genealogical Society), 1960 to date.

Queen City Heritage (formerly *Bulletin of the Cincinnati Historical Society* and *Bulletin of the Historical and Philosophical Society of Ohio*), 1943 to date.

The Tallow Light (Washington County), 1967 to date.

The Tracer (Hamilton County), 1979 to date.

Western Reserve Historical Society Publications. 111 nos., 1870-1929.

WISCONSIN

While Wisconsin holdings of The Newberry Library are not as strong as those for some of the other midwestern states, there is very good material on description and travel, boosterism, emigrant guides, gazetteers, ethnic groups, and frontier and pioneer life. The local history holdings are good for nineteenth-century works, and very good for recent publications. Historical and genealogical bibliographies and guides exist for several counties. The collection of genealogical source material consists primarily of cemetery transcriptions, newspaper abstracts, marriages, and some vital records. These holdings are not extensive, but represent good coverage of what has appeared in print.

The State Historical Society of Wisconsin has long been a leader in the field of state and local history, and its publications are of great importance to researchers. Among the large number of Society publications at the Newberry are all the various publication series; the *Proceedings of the State Historical Society of Wisconsin,* 34th-100th annual meeting (1887-1946); *Wisconsin Magazine of History* (1917+); *Collections of the State Historical Society of Wisconsin,* 31 volumes (1855-1931), which includes many documentary sources such as some vital records from the time of the British regime recorded at Mackinac, and early census records; and *Wisconsin Necrology* (1976). The last item is an index to the obituary file at the Society, covering the years 1846-1944.

Other useful sources include *The Territorial Papers of the United States,* volumes 27 and 28 on Wisconsin Territory, and volumes 10 to 12 on Michigan Territory for the period when Wisconsin was part of Michigan Territory (1818-36); the 1905 state census of Wisconsin on microfilm; and *Wisconsin Blue Book,* useful for information on government officials, politics, and state institutions. The Newberry has thirty scattered volumes between the years 1863 and 1956. There is a biographical index to the *Blue Books.*

Bibliographies and Guides

Margaret Gleason. *Printed Resources for Genealogical Searching in Wisconsin: A Selective Bibliography,* 1964. Good, but not annotated.

Carol Ward Ryan. *Searching for Your Wisconsin Ancestors in the Wisconsin Libraries*, 1979. Good, with helpful bibliographies.

Leroy Schlinkert. *Subject Bibliography of Wisconsin History,* 1947. Emphasizes popular and more accessible references. Many titles not included. No annotations.

Betty Owens Swift. "Genealogical Research in Wisconsin." *National Genealogical Society Quarterly* 68 (December 1980): 270-85. Emphasizes original records and unpublished sources.

Periodical and Serial Publications
Milwaukee History, 1978 to date.

The Peninsula (Door County Historical Society). 9 vols., 1948-71.

Peninsula Historical Review (Door County). 8 vols., 1927-35.

Pierce County's Heritage, 1971 to date.

Collections of the State Historical Society of Wisconsin. 31 vols., 1855-1931.

Wisconsin Families. 4 issues, 1940-41.

Wisconsin Helper. 7 vols., 1967-74.

Wisconsin Lutheran Quarterly. 44 vols., 1904-47.

Wisconsin Magazine of History, 1917 to date.

CHAPTER 15

THE GREAT PLAINS

One of the strengths of The Newberry Library is its holdings of Western Americana, largely due to the Edward E. Ayer and Everett D. Graff collections. Researchers should read Chapter 16, "The Far West," in conjunction with this chapter, because the division of the western states into the Great Plains and the Far West is only one of many ways in which the West can be divided, and because many bibliographies and guides use different designations, such as the Pacific Northwest, the Southwest or the Rocky Mountain West. The published library catalogues to three major Western Americana collections are useful bibliographic sources and are listed at the end of this chapter, along with other guides and bibliographies.

The Newberry and Yale University Library were contributors to the massive microfilm publication, *Western Americana: Frontier History of the Trans-Mississippi West, 1550-1900.* The 617 microfilm reels that make up this publication contain over 7,000 titles reproduced in their entirety from the Yale and Newberry collections. Only printed material is included. The Newberry Card Catalogue does not contain separate catalogue cards for each of the 7,000 individual titles that make up the microfilm publication. About one third of the titles in *Western Americana* are new to the Newberry collection. To determine which titles are included, see *Western Americana: Frontier History of the Trans-Mississippi West, 1550-1900: Guide and Index to the Microfilm Edition,* 2 volumes (1981-82), edited by Archibald Hanna.

Researchers interested in the Great Plains will find abundant material on the period of exploration and discovery and the frontier and pioneer period. The collection is very strong in description and travel accounts, emigrant guides, and works on gold discoveries and mining. Good material is also available on mountain men and the fur trade and ranching and the cattle industry, including many brand books. The collection of local histories is uneven, good for some states, rather weak for others. In general, the collection's strength is its book-length histories. For most of the Great Plains states, researchers will find very little genealogical source material such as church and cemetery records, transcripts of vital records, marriage, probate and deed records, and indexes and transcripts from newspapers. In many cases, this is because little has been available in print.

Bibliographies and Guides
Ramon F. Adams. *Burs Under the Saddle: A Second Look at Books and Histories of the West,* 1964.

_____. *More Burs Under the Saddle,* 1979.

_____. *Six-Guns and Saddle Leather; A Bibliography of Books and Pamphlets on Western Outlaws and Gunmen,* 1954.

Henry R. Wagner. *The Plains and the Rockies: A Critical Bibliography of Exploration, Adventure and Travel in the American West, 1800-1865.* 4th ed., revised, enlarged, and edited by Robert H. Becker, 1982.

Oscar O. Winther. *A Classified Bibliography of the Periodical Literature of the Trans-Mississippi West, 1811-1957,* 1961. Plus *A Supplement (1957-67),* 1970.

Published Library Catalogues
The Bancroft Library, University of California Berkeley, Catalog of Printed Books. 22 vols. plus 3 suppls., 1964-79.

Catalog of the Western History Department, Denver Public Library. 7 vols., 1970.

Catalog of the Yale Collection of Western Americana. 4 vols., 1961.

COLORADO

The history of Colorado has been influenced by the Indians, the Spanish, frontiersmen, prospectors, ranchers, and farmers. Researchers will find a good collection of state and local history material at the Newberry. The library has a very good collection of description and travel accounts, emigrant guides and gazetteers for the pioneer period, as well as a very fine collection of early works on the gold discoveries.

Included in the holdings are a number of rare and significant volumes: *Ein Ausflug Nach den Felsen-Gebirgen im Jahre 1839* (1840), by Adolphus Wislizenus; *Early-Day Letters from Auraria (Now Denver)*

(1907), by Libeus Barney; *Leadville, Colorado: The Most Wonderful Mining Camp in the World! A City only Two Years Old! With Twenty Thousand People, A Complete System of Water Works, and all Modern Improvements* (1879); *The Gold Mines of Western Kansas...* (1858), by William B. Parsons, which is the first edition of the first Pike's Peak gold mines guidebook; *A Trip to Pike's Peak and Notes By the Way* (1861), by Charles M. Clark, one of the best contemporary accounts of the Pike's Peak Gold Rush; and the rare guidebook *Guide to the Kansas Gold Mines at Pike's Peak, Describing the Routes, Camping Places, Tools, Outfits, & C....* (1859), attributed to J. W. Gunnison.

The library's holdings are good for book-length local histories, both old and new, including the first history of Denver, Junius Wharton's *History of the City of Denver* (1866). The collection is much weaker for pamphlet histories and there is little in the way of printed genealogical records, except for what has appeared over the years in *The Colorado Genealogist* and the *Boulder Genealogical Society Quarterly*. The Colorado Genealogical Society has published *Colorado Families: A Territorial Heritage* (1981), a genealogical compilation of those whose ancestors settled in the state prior to 1877. Good material on land companies and their colonization efforts in Colorado will be found, as well as a number of brand books and works on ranching.

Several interesting sources of local and family history information deserve mention. Colorado was one of five states and territories that elected to take an 1885 census with federal assistance. The Newberry has the population, mortality, manufacturing, and agricultural schedules for that census, which contain information similar to that found on the 1880 federal census schedules. An interesting source on early settlements and Indian relations is the first twelve annual reports of the Missionary Bishops of the Episcopal Church of Colorado and Wyoming for the years 1866 to 1878. The library also has *Out West; A Monthly Magazine of Original and Selected Articles, Bearing Principally on the Rocky Mountain Section,* new series, volumes 1-6/7 (July 1873-December 1873/January 1874).

Bibliographies and Guides

Catalog of the Western History Department, Denver Public Library. 7 vols., 1970. This well-known collection covers all of the West, not just Colorado.

Florence Clint. *Colorado Area Key,* 1968. Basic information for genealogists.

Bohdan S. Wynar. *Colorado Bibliography,* 1980. Very good classified bibliography, although it does not include periodical articles. Supersedes *Colorado: A Selected Bibliography of its Literature, 1858-1952* (1954), by Virginia Lee Wilcox.

Periodical and Serial Publications

Boulder Genealogical Society Quarterly, 1969 to date.

The Colorado Genealogist, 1939 to date.

Colorado Heritage, 1981 to date. Supersedes *Colorado Magazine,* 57 vols., 1923-80.

Colorado Historical Society. *Essays and Monographs in Colorado History,* 1983 to date.

University of Colorado Historical Collections. 4 vols., 1918-1941.

THE DAKOTAS

Because their histories are so closely intertwined, both North and South Dakota will be treated together in this chapter. Researchers should check entries in the Card Catalogue under "North Dakota," "South Dakota," "Dakota," and "Dakota Territory." The Newberry's holdings on the Dakotas are fair to good. A number of early and/or rare items are found in the collection, including Charles Collins' *History and Directory of the Black Hills* (1878), one of the first books printed in the Black Hills and one of a handful of extant copies; and Moses K. Armstrong's *History and Resources of Dakota, Montana and Idaho* (1866), the first history of the Dakotas.

A little more than half of the older book-length local histories are found at the library, but few pamphlet histories. The collection is stronger for more recent local histories issued to commemorate county and town centennials. A great deal of travel and description literature is available, including promotional tracts and emigrant guides. The territorial period is well covered, and there is a good collection of pamphlets on the Dakotas' struggle to gain statehood. Much material on army posts will be found, and many of these items include maps and plans of forts. One important example from the Graff collection is "Collection of General Orders and Circulares, 1867-1874. U. S. Army, Department of Dakota." Published papers from the Dakota History Conferences, beginning with the first conference in 1969, are also available.

Genealogical source material is quite meager. Only a few works, mostly marriage records and cemetery transcriptions, will be found. The library does have the Fargo, North Dakota, and Moorhead, Minnesota, city directories from 1881-1927 on microfiche. Dakota Territory was one of only five states and territories which opted to take an 1885 census with federal assistance. This 1885 census is transcribed in *Collections of the State Historical Society of North Dakota,* volume 4 (1913).

Bibliographies and Guides

Herbert T. Hoover, ed. *Planning for the South Dakota Centennial: A Bibliography,* 1984. A selective guide to "the best" literature on various aspects of South Dakota history.

Leonard Jennewein. *Black Hills Booktrails,* 1962.

Sue Laubersheimer. *South Dakota: Changing, Changeless, 1889-1989: A Selected Annotated Bibliography,* 1985. An excellent guide to books, articles, maps, and audio-visual materials.

Watson Parker. "A Black Hills Bibliography." *South Dakota Historical Collections* 35 (1970): 169-301.

Dan Rylance. *Reference Guide to North Dakota History,* 1979. Very good, includes many periodical articles.

Lesta Van Der Wert Turchen and James D. McLaird. *County and Community: A Bibliography of South Dakota Local Histories,* 1979. Very good, annotated guide to books and articles.

Periodical and Serial Publications

Bits and Pieces. 12 vols., 1965-80.

Black Hills Nuggets (Rapid City Society for Genealogical Research), 1968 to date.

Collections of the State Historical Society of North Dakota. 7 vols., 1906-25.

North Dakota History (formerly *North Dakota Historical Quarterly*), 1926 to date.

The Record (Fargo). 9 vols., 1895-1904. "Historical, Personal and Other Sketches, Politics, Literature and Education, Social and Fraternal Affairs."

Red River Valley Historian. Vols. 2-12, 1968-78.

South Dakota Historical Collections, 1902 to date.

South Dakota History, 1970 to date.

The South Dakotan. 7 vols., 1898-1904. "A Monthly Magazine Devoted to Dakota History, Literature, Art and Progress."

Wi-Iyohi (South Dakota Historical Society). 24 vols., 1947-70.

IDAHO

The Newberry Library's holdings for Idaho are among the weakest for the western states. Although the library has a good collection of book-length local histories, it lacks many of the pamphlets in which much Idaho local history has appeared. There is little material on the timber industry and agriculture, and limited material on the fur trade. With the exception of a few cemetery records, there is virtually no genealogical source material such as transcripts of vital records, deeds, probates, and church records.

The library does have many description and travel accounts of early Idaho, and good material on the gold fields, including Frederick Fry's *Traveller's Guide, and Descriptive Journal of the Great North-Western Territories of the United States of America...* (1865), the earliest account of the Idaho and Montana mines. Several Idaho brand books, including the first one published in 1885, are part of the library collection. Researchers will also find some material on the Mormon penetration of early Idaho.

Some local history material (the article "Idaho Town Names," for example), is found in the *Biennial Report of Idaho State Historical Society,* volumes 6-24 (1917/18-1953/54). *The Idaho Encyclopedia* (1938), a publication of the Federal Writers' Project of the WPA, is another source that provides ready-reference help, although some of the information is outdated.

Bibliographies and Guides

Richard W. Etulain and Merwin Swanson. *Idaho History: A Bibliography,* 1976. Good listing of books, pamphlets, and periodical articles, although not annotated.

Milo G. Nelson and Charles A. Webbert. *Idaho Local History: A Bibliography with a Checklist of Library Holdings,* 1976. Includes books and pamphlets only.

Periodical and Serial Publications

Idaho Yesterdays, 1957 to date.

Owyhee Outpost (Owyhee County), 1970 to date.

Snake River Echoes (Upper Snake River Valley Historical Society), 1971 to date.

KANSAS

Researchers interested in Kansas and Kansans will find a good collection, on a variety of topics, at The Newberry Library. Three volumes of annals have been published and are invaluable sources for local historians, genealogists, social historians, and other researchers. Daniel W. Wilder's *The Annals of Kansas,* new ed. (1886), covers the years 1540-1885. This volume is continued by Jennie S. Owen's *The Annals of Kansas, 1886-1925,* 2 volumes (1956). The books contain a day-by-day chronology of events taken from newspapers and official sources. In addition to the many names that appear, much social history can be gleaned. For example, the 4 February 1882 entry reports "The roller skating mania rages."

A companion volume and very important source book is Louise Barry's *The Beginning of the West: Annals of the Kansas Gateway to the American West, 1540-1854* (1972). Barry's book attempts to chronicle all known activity in pre-statehood Kansas and includes entries on Spanish explorers, the French, military personnel, trappers, traders, missionaries, wagon trains, and more. Sources include newspapers, travel accounts, and military dispatches. Information on wagon trains to the West is very difficult to locate, and this book may provide some help, since many wagon trains passed through the towns and military forts of Kansas. An example is this entry for mid-May 1853: "The California-bound emigrant company headed by Charles Albright, which included John B. Haas, arrived at the Big Blue crossing (present Marysville)..." (p. 1153).

The Newberry has a very good collection of book-length local histories, including many published in recent years for the U. S. Bicentennial and Kansas town and county centennials. The collection is very strong in travel accounts and emigrants' guides, and includes such rarities as J. Butler Chapman's *History of Kansas: An Emigrant's Guide* (1855) and Edward H. Hale's *Kanzas* [sic] *and Nebraska: The History, Geographical and Physical Characteristics, And Political Position of Those Territories...* (1854). Much material is available on the territorial period, the Border Wars, Bleeding Kansas, early pioneer history, ranching, accounts of military personnel, and the settlement of free Blacks in Kansas towns. In 1856 the U. S. House of Representatives appointed a Committee to Investigate the Troubles in Kansas. The committee's report is found in volume 869 of the *U. S. Serial Set*. It includes testimony from witnesses, poll books, voter registers, and other lists containing names. Some personal information, such as the date an individual came to Kansas, is often recorded. Robert A. Hodge has prepared *An Index to the Report of the Special Committee Appointed to Investigate the Troubles in Kansas 1856* (1984).

Some transcripts of genealogical source material will be found, mostly cemetery records and marriages, although a small number of deed records, probates, and vital statistics records are available. Microfilm publications of the papers of two Indian missionaries--"The Isaac McCoy Papers, 1808-1874" and "The Jotham Meeker Papers, 1825-1864"--provide information, not only on Indians and Indian missions, but also on early pioneer life. Both of these papers are from the Kansas State Historical Society. The library also has the newspaper the *Lawrence Republican* for May 1857 to November 1862.

The Kansas State Historical Society has produced numerous valuable books on state and local history, including the *Annals* mentioned above. Nearly all of these works will be found at the library. Among these are *Publications of the Kansas Historical Society,* 3 volumes (1886-1930); *Biennial Report of the Board of Directors,* 1st, 5th-27th (1878/79, 1885/86-1929/30); and *Collections of the Kansas State Historical Society,* 17 volumes (1881-1928). There is a comprehensive index to these latter three series.

Bibliographies and Guides
Lorene Anderson and A. W. Farley. "A Bibliography of Town and County Histories of Kansas." *Kansas Historical Quarterly* 21 (Autumn 1955): 513-51. Good list of books and pamphlets.

Mary B. Curtis. "Bibliography of Kansas: The Formative Years." *Magazine of Bibliographies* 1 (December 1972): 9-39. Good.

Periodical and Serial Publications
Heritage Genealogical Society Quarterly (Wilson County), 1971 to date.

In the Beginning (Woodson County), 1968 to date.

Kansas History (formerly *Kansas Historical Quarterly*), 1931 to date.

Shawnee County Historical Society Bulletin, 1946 to date.

The Treesearcher (Kansas Genealogical Society), 1962 (vol. 4) to date.

NOTES
1. Daniel W. Wilder, *The Annals of Kansas* (Topeka: T. D. Thacher, 1886), p. 963.

MONTANA

The Montana holdings of The Newberry Library are rather meager, although researchers will find most of the standard works on state history. The collection of local histories is weak, and there is very little genealogical source material. Some information can be found on pioneer life, ranching, mines, gold and silver fields, and some description and travel accounts, and reminiscences.

The library does have several Montana brand books; the University of Montana Publications in History series (1971+), which deals with state and local history; the series Montana and the West (1983+); *Contributions of the Historical Society of Montana,* 10 volumes (1876-1941); and a number of collective biographies and "mug books" containing biographical sketches of early Montana residents. One important volume is *Society of Montana Pioneers. Constitution, Members, and Officers, with Portraits and Maps* (1899), with its several hundred short sketches of Montana pioneers.

Bibliographies and Guides
Coburn Johnson. *Bibliography of Montana Local Histories,* 1977. Good.

Dennis Lee Richards. *Montana's Genealogical and Local History Records,* 1981. Contains extensive bibliographies of church and family histories, and a detailed source list for each county.

Periodical and Serial Publications
Bits and Pieces. 12 vols., 1965-80.

Frontier and Midland; A Magazine of the Northwest. 19 vols., 1920-39.

Montana, the Magazine of Western History, 1951 to date.

NEBRASKA

Local historians will find a fair to good collection of Nebraska material at The Newberry Library, while genealogists will find the holdings to be rather weak. The collection is best for the period from the explorations of Lewis and Clark in 1804 to the end of the territorial period in 1867. A large number of description and travel accounts will be found, as well as pioneer reminiscences, including two volumes of *Reminiscences and Proceedings, Nebraska Territorial Pioneers' Association* (1917-23).

For the territorial period there are Journals of the Nebraska Territory Legislative Assembly, council sessions 1-5 and 8-12 (1855-58, 1861-67), and Journals of the Territory Legislative Assembly, House of Representatives, sessions 3-6 and 8-11 (1856-59, 1861-66). The library has a good collection of the older local histories, including such rarities as *Descriptive Pamphlet of Knox County, Nebraska* (1883), by E. A. Fry and a fair collection of newer book-length local histories. Little genealogical source material will be found, with the exception of a few cemetery and marriage records, and material from Nebraska genealogical periodicals.

Bibliographies and Guides
Myrtle D. Berry. "Local Nebraska History--A Bibliography." *Nebraska History* 26 (April-June 1945): 104-15. Lists books and pamphlets only. Is incomplete but does include the major works.

Nebraska State Genealogical Society. *Nebraska: A Guide to Genealogical Research,* 1984.

John Browning White. *Published Sources on Territorial Nebraska: An Essay and Bibliography,* 1956. Very fine annotated listing of books and articles. Works published after the territorial period are included, so many of the references do contain information on post-

1867 Nebraska.

Periodical and Serial Publications

Nebraska Ancestree (Nebraska Genealogical Society), 1978 to date.

The Nebraska and Midwest Genealogical Record. 22 vols., 1923-44.

Nebraska History, 1918 to date.

Nebraska State Historical Society Bulletin, 1965 to date.

Publications of the Nebraska State Historical Society, 1885 to date.

Roots and Leaves (Eastern Nebraska Genealogical Society), 1983 (vol. 6) to date.

NEW MEXICO

The Newberry Library has a good collection of material on New Mexico, including works on Spanish exploration, travel accounts and personal narratives, the U. S. military presence, gunfighters, the Lincoln County Range War, guidebooks for settlers, and early maps. The holdings on the Spanish period include such important accounts as *Memorial Qve Fray Ivan de Santander...* by Alonso de Benavides (1630) and Augustin de Vetancurt's *Chronica de la Provincia Del Santo Evangelio de Mexico...En Mexico...* (1697).

The library has two microfilm sets entitled *Spanish Archives of New Mexico.* One contains ten reels, the other, twenty-three reels. Readers are cautioned that the two sets are different. Both sets are accompanied by printed guides--one set appears in the main Card Catalogue, while the other is listed in the New Catalogue. Some other series and collections found at the Newberry include *Publications of the Quivera Society,* 13 volumes (1929-58); *Publications of the Historical Society of New Mexico,* 29 volumes (1881-1924) (volumes 1 and 5 are missing); and Historical Society of New Mexico, Publications in History, 15 volumes (1926-54).

A number of the Spanish and Mexican censuses are available, as well as increasing amounts of material on Spanish and Mexican land grants (including some in what is now Colorado). For information on early New Mexico families, researchers should consult *Origins of New Mexico Families in the Spanish Colonial Period* (1973), by Angelico Chavez, which covers the period 1598-1821. Very few marriage, birth, death, probate, or cemetery records will be found. The library does have the New Mexico Local Histories Series by Stanley Francis Louis Crocchiola (pseud., F. Stanley). This series of 109 popular booklets, published between 1960 and 1970, often represents the only written account of an area. Each booklet can be found in the Card Catalogue under the name of the locale.

Bibliographies and Guides

Christine Buder Myers. *New Mexico Local and County Histories: A Bibliography,* 1983. Good. Few annotations; most periodical articles are excluded.

Lyle Saunders. *A Guide to Materials Bearing on Cultural Relations in New Mexico,* 1944. Lists published and manuscript materials on Spanish-Americans, Indians, and Anglos, although many of the entries are of a sociological nature.

Wilma Loy Shelton. *Checklist of New Mexico Publications, 1850-1953,* 1954.

Frances Leon Swadesh. *A New Mexico Bibliography,* 1973.

Periodical and Serial Publications

New Mexico Historical Review, 1926 to date.

Old Santa Fe. 3 vols., 1913-16.

Rio Grande History. 11 vols., 1973-79.

OKLAHOMA

Prior to statehood Oklahoma was made up of Indian Territory and Oklahoma Territory, and researchers should be sure to check Card Catalogue entries under "Oklahoma," "Oklahoma Territory," and "Indian Territory." The Newberry has good holdings of description and travel accounts, settlers' guides, works on ranching and the cattle industry, the opening of Oklahoma to settlement, and the statehood question. The collection of local histories is fair, and there are some early marriage records, cemetery records, and other genealogical source material, although the collection is not strong. The exception to this is the excellent collection on American Indian genealogy, which is covered in Chapter 5.

For those interested in ethnic and racial groups, the University of Oklahoma Press has published a series, "Newcomers to a New Land," with volumes on blacks, British and Irish, Czechs, Germans, Germans from Russia, Indians, Italians, Jews, Mexicans, and Poles. The Oklahoma Historical Society publishes the "Oklahoma Series" (1975+), which covers a variety of topics on state history. The Newberry has the Special Publications of the Oklahoma Genealogical Society, beginning with volume 2 (1969+), which include works on veterans, censuses, and cemeteries. Also available on microfilm is *A Compilation of Records from the Choctaw Nation, Indian Territory* (1976), which deals mostly with Indians in the pre-statehood period, but does include some non-Indians. This compilation, by the Oklahoma Genealogical Society, includes the 1896 Choctaw Nation Census, cemetery, church, and marriage records, and other miscellaneous records.

Bibliographies and Guides

Edward Everett Dale and Morris L. Wardell. *Outline and References for Oklahoma History*. 4th ed., 1936. Not annotated.

Anne Hodges Morgan. *Oklahoma Image Materials Guide,* 1981. Good, selective bibliography with lengthy annotations. It has no specific chapter on local or county histories.

Periodical and Serial Publications

Chronicles of Oklahoma, 1921 to date.

Oklahoma Genealogical Society Quarterly, 1955 to date.

The Oklahoma Pontotoc County Quarterly. 10 vols., 1969-78.

Prairie Lore (Southwestern Oklahoma Historical Society), 1964 to date.

Red River Valley Historical Review. 7 vols., 1974-82.

Tulsa Annals (Tulsa Genealogical Society). 13 vols., 1966-78.

TEXAS

The colorful and diverse history of Texas is reflected in the tremendous amount of material written about the state. The Newberry holdings, although far from comprehensive, do provide solid background materials and sources for the study of Texas state and local history. The collection is particularly good for the Spanish and Mexican periods. Included in the holdings are Alvar Nuñez Cabeza de Vaca's *La Relacion y Comentarios del Gouernador Aluar Nuñez Cabeza de Vaca,...* (1555), the first printed book about Texas, and Juan Antonio de la Pena's *Derrotero de la Expedicion en la Provincia de los Texas* (1722), a good source about Texas as a Spanish province. The holdings are also good for the Texas Revolution, the Republic of Texas (1836-45), the annexation of Texas, reminiscences, personal narratives, and traveller's and emigrant's guides, such as *Guide to the Republic of Texas...* (1839), by Richard S. Hunt and Jesse F. Randel, the first general guide to the state.

Researchers will also find much material on various colonization movements and promotional literature from companies encouraging immigration. One interesting example is *Memorial que Varios Ciudadanos de los Estados-Unidos de America,...* (1822), by The Texas Association, a petition relating to the founding of the Robertson Colony, one of the earliest attempts by American citizens to colonize Mexican Texas. Some information is also available on the Texas Rangers, although more can be found on badmen and outlaws.

For local histories, the Newberry collection is strongest for the Spanish areas, East Texas and the Gulf areas. The holdings of local and county histories are fair to good. There is some material on ethnic groups, especially German immigrants to the state. Some genealogical compilations of marriage, land, probate, and cemetery records will be found, although Newberry researchers will find little or nothing on many of Texas's 254 counties. The library does have the Mortality Schedules for the census years 1850-80. Texas was part of the Confederacy, and the Newberry has the Freedmen's Bureau Field Office Records, which provide much information on blacks in nineteenth-century Texas.

Other sources of interest are *Publications of the Quivera Society,* 13 volumes (1929-58), a few of which deal with Texas; the annual *The Texas Almanac...with Statistics, Descriptive and Biographical Sketches, etc., Relating to Texas* (1857-73); and short runs of three early Texas newspapers: *Dallas Herald* (1866-70), *San Antonio Express* (1868-74), and *San Antonio Herald* (1855-63).

Bibliographies and Guides

Horace B. Carroll. *Texas County Histories,* 1943. Good.

Catalog of the Texas Collection in the Barker Texas History Center, The University of Texas at Austin. 14 vols., 1979.

John H. Jenkins. *Basic Texas Books: An Annotated Bibliography of Selected Works for a Research Library,* 1983. Excludes most local and county histories.

_____. *Cracker Barrel Chronicles: A Bibliography of Texas Town and County Histories,* 1965. Very good list of books, pamphlets, articles, theses, and dissertations. Not annotated.

Tom Munnerlyn. *Texas Local History,* 1983. List of local histories and genealogical records currently for sale.

Caldwell W. Raines. *A Bibliography of Texas,* 1896. Still useful, annotated.

Thomas W. Streeter. *Bibliography of Texas: 1795-1845.* 2nd ed., revised and enlarged, 1983. Very good, quite detailed.

Periodical and Serial Publications

Chronicles of Smith County, 1963 (vol. 2) to date.

Dallas Genealogical Society Quarterly, 1957 (vol. 3) to date.

East Texas Historical Journal, 1963 to date.

Frontier Times. 31 vols., 1923-54.

Hale County History, 1971 to date.

Hays County Historical and Genealogical Society Quarterly. 12 vols., 1967-78.

Houston Review. 4 vols., 1979-82.

Military History of Texas and the Southwest, 1961 to date.

North Texas Pioneer. 8 vols., 1966-73.

Password (El Paso County), 1969 (vol. 14) to date.

Permian Historical Annual. 13 vols., 1961-73.

Southwestern Historical Quarterly (formerly the *Quarterly of the Texas State Historical Association*), 1897 to date.

Stirpes (Texas Genealogical Society), 1961 to date.

Texana (Waco). 12 vols., 1963-74.

Texas Gulf Historical and Biographical Record, 1965 to date.

West Texas Historical Association Yearbook, 1925 to date.

Yellowed Pages (Southeast Texas Genealogical and Historical Society), 1971 to date.

WYOMING

Wyoming, which sits partly in the Rocky Mountains and partly on the Great Plains, has been the scene of much activity in ranching and min-. ing. The Newberry's Wyoming collection lacks some of the bibliographic tools on Wyoming state and local history, and the collection of local histories is poor. Although all the standard state histories are available, the holdings of genealogical source material are quite meager. Most of the collection deals with the frontier and pioneer period, and there are some description and travel accounts, guidebooks and emigrant guides, and materials on ranching, the cattle industry, and brand books. One useful manuscript source from the Everett D. Graff collection is 240 letters (1891-98) from Robert M. Divine, a foreman on the CK Ranch near Casper, reporting on the daily operation of a Wyoming ranch.

The Newberry does have *Collections of the Wyoming Historical Society* (1897); *Miscellanies of the Wyoming Historical Society* (1919); and the journals *Bits and Pieces,* 12 volumes (1965-80); and *Annals of Wyoming* (1923+).

Bibliographies and Guides
Rose Mary Malone. *Wyomingana: Two Bibliographies,* 1950. Contains books only.

Virginia Cole Trenholm, ed. *Wyoming Blue Book.* 3 vols., vols. 1 and 2 published 1946, reprinted with vol. 3, 1974. Good reference source.

Contains some state history, brief histories of counties, government facts, biographies, election returns, and documentary material.

CHAPTER 16

THE FAR WEST

The Newberry Library is acknowledged as one of the country's leading libraries for the study of the American West. Most of the material on the Far West is found in the Everett D. Graff and Edward E. Ayer collections. Researchers interested in the states of the Far West should also read Chapter 15, "The Great Plains," because many of the sources discussed cover both sections of the country.

The areas of strength on the far western states vary, but in general researchers will find excellent holdings of description and travel literature, emigrant guides, gazetteers and maps, and good material on the U. S. military presence and frontier and pioneer life. One interesting example from the Graff collection that combines maps and the military is "Outline Descriptions of Military Posts in the Military Division of the Pacific" (1879), which consists of maps of sixty-eight military posts in Arizona Territory, California, Idaho Territory, Nevada, Oregon and Washington Territory.

The Newberry has strong holdings of bibliographies and library catalogues on the Far West. Several of the most important ones are listed below. One useful source for biographical information is Joseph G. Drazan's *The Pacific Northwest: An Index to People and Places in Books* (1979), a selective index to 320 books providing information on 6,830 people and 2,100 places. The holdings of genealogical source material for most of the Far Western states are quite meager, while the amount of state and local histories varies from state to state.

Bibliographies and Guides

Charles W. Smith. *Pacific Northwest Americana.* 3rd ed., 1950, plus 1981 supplement. Very important. Covers Idaho, Montana, Oregon, Washington, British Columbia, Alaska, and the Yukon. No subject index.

Henry R. Wagner. *The Spanish Southwest, 1542-1794, An Annotated Bibliography,* 1937.

The footnotes and bibliographies in Hubert Bancroft's histories of the West are still useful.

Library Catalogues

The Dictionary Catalog of the Pacific Northwest Collection, University of Washington Libraries, Seattle. 6 vols., 1972.

Dictionary Catalogue of the Provincial Archives of British Columbia, Victoria. 8 vols., 1971.

Selected Series

University of Utah, Publications in the American West, 1969 (vol. 2) to date.

Western Frontier Library, 1953 to date.

Western Frontiersmen Series, 1937 to date.

Selected Journals

Frontier and Midland, A Magazine of the Northwest. 19 vols., 1920-39.

Hispanic American Historical Review, 1918 to date.

Journal of the West, 1962 to date.

Pacific Historian, 1957 to date.

Pacific Northwest Quarterly, 1906 to date.

The Record (Friends of the Library, Washington State University). 39 vols., 1938-78.

Southwestern Historical Quarterly (formerly the *Quarterly of the Texas State Historical Association*), 1897 to date.

Western Historical Quarterly, 1969 to date.

Western Humanities Review, 27 vols, 1947-73.

Western States Jewish Historical Quarterly, 1968 to date.

ALASKA

The Newberry's holdings are strong for the exploration and early settlement of America's last frontier--Alaska, largely because the Edward E. Ayer collection is very strong for works on the northwest coast. The Russians in Alaska and the activities of the Russian-American Company are well covered, as are missions and missionary activities by various church denominations. Many description and travel accounts from the eighteenth century through the early twentieth century are also available.

The library has good holdings concerning the Alaska Gold Rush and the gold fields, including many maps. A source that complements the Gold Rush material is the 1900 Federal Population Census Schedules for Alaska. These are especially interesting because the format differs from the rest of the 1900 schedules. A column headed "Post-Office Address at Home" appears, and most people listed their prior residence in the continental U. S. There is also a small collection of local histories, including ones for Fairbanks, Juneau, Nome, Sitka, and Skagway.

Several good bibliographies and guides are devoted to Alaska state and local history, making the state one of the best covered bibliographically. These are listed below. The library also has several serial publications, including Historical Monographs of the Alaska State Library (1970+); a few publications from the Alaska Historical Commission Studies in History; and a series published by Limestone Press known both as "Alaska History" and "Materials for the Study of Alaska History" (1972+). Twenty-seven volumes have been published to date, and many deal with the Russian-American Company.

The Newberry has some early magazines and newspapers: *Alaska-Yukon Magazine.*, 13 volumes (1905-12) and a facsimile in both English and Russian of *The Alaska Herald* (1868-74). *Subject Index to the Alaskan, 1885-1907, a Sitka Newspaper* (1974), by Robert N. DeArmond, is also available, although the library does not have the newspaper itself.

Bibliographies and Guides

Alaska Historical Commission. *Writing Alaska's History: A Guide to Research.* Volume 1, 1974. Contains articles on historiography, and bibliographical aids and sources.

Arctic Institute of North America. *Arctic Bibliography.* 12 vols., 1953-65. Mostly devoted to natural history, but includes some material on explorations.

Stephen W. Haycox and Betty J. Haycox. *Melvin Ricks' Bibliography: An Introductory Guide to Alaskan Historical Literature,* 1977. Good annotated guide to books, pamphlets, articles, and government publications.

Elsie A. Tourville. *Alaska: A Bibliography, 1570-1970,* 1974. Includes books only. Not annotated.

James Wickersham. *A Bibliography of Alaska Literature, 1724-1924,* 1927. Still valuable despite its age. Includes books, U. S. government publications, and periodical articles.

Periodical and Serial Publications

Alaska History (Alaska Historical Society), 1984 to date.

The Alaska Journal. 10 vols., 1971-80. "History and Arts of the North."

The Beaver (Hudson's Bay Company), 1935 (issue 266) to date.

ARIZONA

The Newberry's local and family history collection on Arizona is rather weak, although the library does have some interesting transcripts of manuscript material on the Spanish missions and missionaries in Arizona, some published documents from the territorial legislative assembly, and good material on military life, boosterism literature, and description and travel accounts, such as the very rare *Notes of Travel Through the Territory of Arizona* (1870), by John H. Marion, an account of a trip through a previously unexplored area of the state. Much Arizona material is also found in the *U.S. Serial Set* (see Chapter 2).

The Newberry collection is also quite limited for Arizona local histories, although the library does have some of the state and territorial histories, including the first general history of Arizona, Sylvester Mowry's *Memoir of the Proposed Territory of Arizona* (1857). Much of the early information on Arizona appeared not in book form, but in the popular press--newspapers and magazines--and in scientific journals. Two guides to this literature are available. David M. Goodman's *Arizona Odyssey: Bibliographic Adventures in Nineteenth-Century Magazines* (1969) is a very good, briefly annotated guide which includes much scientific material, information on Indians, and travelers' accounts. Although the Newberry lacks most of the scientific journals, the collection is quite good for the literary and popular magazines. The second source is *The Arizona Index: A Subject Index to Periodical Articles About the State* (1978), compiled by Donald M. Powell and Virginia E. Rice.

With the exception of indexes to several federal and territorial censuses from the 1860s and 1870s, there is little genealogical source material in the collection. The library does have an interesting source on Indian and civilian interaction with the military in the U. S. Army Annual Reports of the Department of Arizona, 1874-88 (incomplete).

Bibliographies and Guides

Hector Alliot. *Bibliography of Arizona: Being the Record of Literature Collected by Joseph Amasa Munk, M. D., and Donated by Him to the Southwest Museum of Los Angeles, California,* 1914. The collection, although far from comprehensive, did include many significant early works.

Donald M. Powell. *Arizona Gathering II, 1950-1969: An Annotated Bibliography,* 1973. Includes books, articles, dissertations.

Andrew Wallace. *Sources and Readings in Arizona History,* 1965. Excludes most old and rare items. No annotations.

Periodical and Serial Publications

Arizona and the West, 1959 to date.

Arizona Historical Review. 7 vols., 1928-36.

Arizona Historical Society, Historical Monographs series, 1973 to date.

Arizona Quarterly, 1967 (vol. 23) to date.

The Journal of Arizona History (formerly *Arizoniana*), 1960 to date. Some early issues are missing.

The Smoke Signal (Tucson Corral of the Westerners), 1960 to date.

CALIFORNIA

The allure of California is not a recent phenomenon. California has drawn immigrants, migrants, and settlers since the time of the Gold Rush. Researchers at the Newberry will find a good collection on several aspects of California history: description and travel accounts, Gold Rush literature, the Spanish and Mexican era, missions and missionaries, and ethnic groups in the state. In general, the collection is stronger for northern California than for southern California. The holdings of state and local histories are good, including over half of all published county and local histories. There is a small amount of genealogical source material, consisting mostly of newspaper extracts, vital records, and cemetery transcriptions.

A number of biographical indexes, lists, and guides are available including Marie E. Northrop's *Spanish-Mexican Families of Early California, 1769-1850,* 2 volumes (1976-84); *The Argonauts of California* (1890, reprinted 1975) by Charles Warren Haskins, which covers the Gold Rush period; Nathan C. Parker's *Personal Name Index to the 1856 City Directories of California* (1980), which indexes six directories; and *An Index to the Biographies in the Nineteenth Century California County Histories* (1979) by J. Carlyle Parker, which includes approximately 16,500

entries from forty-seven of California's fifty-eight counties. The Newberry has about seventy-five percent of the titles in this index. Also useful are two series by Louis J. Rasmussen: *Railway Passenger Lists of
Overland Trains to San Francisco and the West* (1966+) and *San Francisco Ship Passenger Lists* (1965+). Both of these are reconstructions
based on newspapers, journals, diaries, letters, and magazines.

Bibliographies and Guides

Hubert H. Bancroft. *History of California.* 7 vols., 1884-90. The bibliographical sections in volume one are still useful.

Robert Ernest Cowan and Robert Grannis Cowan. *A Bibliography of
the History of California, 1510-1930,* 1964. Important listing of about
five thousand books with brief annotations.

Margaret Miller Rocq. *California Local History: A Bibliography and
Union List of Holdings.* 2nd ed., 1970, plus 1976 supplement. Very
good, comprehensive list of books, pamphlets, theses, and dissertations. Includes a large number of regional and state-wide works.

Francis J. Weber. *A Select Bibliographical Guide to California History,
1863-1972,* 1972. A very good bibliography of bibliographies on
various aspects of California history. Includes many articles and
obscure sources.

Special Publications

California Centennial Edition. Vols. 3-22, 1945-50. The library lacks
volumes 8, 15, 18. New writings and reprints on state and local history.

California Historical Society, Special Publications, 1923 to date. Over
fifty volumes have appeared. The Newberry lacks a few. Contents
include journals and diaries, biographies, Gold Rush material, local
history, and travel and exploration accounts.

Historical Society of Southern California, Publications. 16 vols., 1884-
1934.

Publications of the Quivera Society. 13 volumes, 1929-58. Some deal
with California.

Periodical and Serial Publications

California Central Coast Genealogical Society, 1968 to date.

California History, 1922 to date.

California History Nugget. 7 vols., 1928-40.

Chispa (Tuolumne Co.), 1961 to date.

The Covered Wagon (Shasta Historical Society), 1943 (vol. 2) to date. Some early issues are missing.

Quarterly of the Historical Society of Southern California, 1884 to date.

Orange County Genealogical Society Quarterly, 1964 to date.

The Pacific Historian, 1957 to date.

Pacific Historical Review, 1932 to date.

The Pioneer: or California Monthly Magazine. 4 vols., January 1854-December 1855. The first California magazine.

Pomona Valley Historian, 1965 to date.

Pony Express Courier. 35 vols., 1934-69.

Trinity County Historical Society Yearbook, 1955-74.

Valley Trails (Stockton Corral of the Westerners), 1967 to date.

La Vista (San Luis Obispo Co.), 1968 to date.

The Westerner. 5 vols., 1927-31.

HAWAII

Although Hawaii, with its orientation to the Pacific and Asia, differs considerably from the mainland states, Newberry researchers will still find a good collection on the Islands. Most of the material is part of the Edward E. Ayer collection. In addition to his interest in American Indians, Ayer was also interested in the Caribbean Islands, the Philippines, and Hawaii. The holdings are best for the period before 1900, although a small amount of early twentieth century material is available. Researchers should be sure to check the Card Catalogue under the subject headings "Hawaii," "Hawaii (Territory)" for the period after 1900, and "Hawaiian Islands" for the period before 1900.

There is good material on the discovery and early contact with the Sandwich Islands (as Hawaii was earlier known), nineteenth-century travel and description accounts, the annexation of Hawaii, and nineteenth-century Hawaiian magazines and journals. Much is available on missionaries, including many printed journals, diaries, and accounts. Many of the missionary families were from New England, and the journals and accounts often contain genealogical and family information with New England associations. Works and reports of some of the Hawaiian mission societies are available, including the *Annual Reports of the Hawaiian Evangelical Association* (1878-1911, incomplete). The Newberry holdings also include government reports, laws, statutes, and codes (many of which are in the Hawaiian language), and *Hawaiian Almanac and Annual,* "information and statistics on the Territory for merchants, tourists and others," for the years 1877, 1882-1927.

Several sources on Hawaiian genealogies and family lists are available: Edith Kawelohea McKinzie's *Hawaiian Genealogies Extracted from Hawaiian Language Newspapers* (1983+), Milton Rubincam's *America's Only Royal Family: Genealogy of the Former Hawaiian Ruling House* (1968), *An Account of the Polynesian Race,* 3 volumes (1878-85) by Abraham Fornander, and Davida Malo's *Hawaiian Antiquities,* 2nd edition (1951), translated from the 1898 Hawaiian edition. The last two works contain family lists.

Bibliographies and Guides
David J. Kittelson. *The Hawaiians: An Annotated Bibliography,* 1985. Good. Includes books, articles, and theses in English. All subjects are included, but the book is historically oriented.

Nineteenth-Century Journals and Magazines
The Friend, 1843-1954.

The Hawaiian, 1895-96.

The Hawaiian Monthly, 1884.

The Hawaiian Spectator, 1838-39.

The Islander, A Weekly Journal Devoted to Hawaiian Interests, Scientific Researches, Literature, Home and Foreign Affairs, 1875.

Ke Kumu Hawaii, 1834-39.

Sandwich Islands News, 1846-47.

Periodical and Serial Publications
Bernice Pauahi Bishop Museum, Occasional Papers. 24 vols., 1898-1971.

Annual Report of the Hawaiian Historical Society. 88 vols., 1892-1979.

Papers of the Hawaiian Historical Society. 21 numbers, 1892-1940.

The Hawaiian Journal of History, 1967 to date.

Publications of the Historical Commission of the Territory of Hawaii. 6 numbers, 1923-29.

The Mid-Pacific Magazine. 49 vols., 1911-36.

NEVADA

The Newberry Library's Nevada holdings are among the smallest for the far western states, although the collection covers several aspects of Nevada history in some detail. The holdings provide good coverage of the mining era, including many maps of mines and the series *Historic*

Mining Camps of Nevada (1970+). Much material is available on Virginia City as well. There is almost no genealogical source material, largely because very little has been published. For the same reason, there are not a great many county or town histories. The Newberry does have a good collection of those that have appeared, as well as nearly all the general histories of the state. The library also has a fair to good collection of description and travel accounts, some secondary material on ghost towns, some early directories, and a printed copy of the 1875 Nevada State Census.

Bibliographies and Guides
Russell R. Elliott and Helen J. Poulton. *Writings on Nevada: A Selected Bibliography*, 1963. A good, but unannotated work including books, articles, theses, and dissertations.

Stanley W. Paher. *Nevada: An Annotated Bibliography*, 1980. Very good list of books, pamphlets, theses, and dissertations.

Periodical and Serial Publications
Nevada Historical Review. 3 vols., 1973-75.

Nevada Historical Society Biennial Report. 1st-11th, 1907/08-1927/28.

Nevada Historical Society Quarterly, 1958 (vol. 2) to date.

Northeastern Nevada Historical Society Quarterly, 1970 to date.

Papers of the Nevada Historical Society. 5 vols., 1913/16-1925/26.

OREGON

The Newberry Library has a good collection on Oregon, especially for the pioneer and settlement periods. Included are many early emigrant guides such as Hall J. Kelley's *A Geographical Sketch of that Part of North America, Called Oregon...* (1830), Lansford W. Hastings' *The Emigrants' Guide to Oregon and California...* (1845), and Joel Palmer's *Journal of Travels over the Rocky Mountains, to the Mouth of the Columbia River...* (1847). The library also holds a copy of the first printed account of the first emigrant party to cross the plains, John B. Wyeth's *Oregon; Or, a Short History of a Long Journey from the Atlantic Ocean to the Region of the Pacific,...* (1833). There is much material on the overland route to Oregon, pioneer settlement, personal narratives and reminiscences, missions and missionaries to the Indians, and the Oregon Question. Many works of a promotional/boosterism nature are also part of the collection. The local history holdings are fair, but there is little genealogical source material, with the important exception of *Genealogical Material in Oregon Donation Land Claims* (1957-67), compiled by the Genealogical Forum of Portland. This four-volume set includes both accepted and rejected claims filed at the land offices in Oregon City, Roseburg, and The Dalles.

The Newberry holds several other items of interest to Oregon researchers: the Oregon Territorial Census of Males over twenty-one for 1849, on microfilm; transactions of the first to fifty-sixth annual reunions (1873-1928) of the Oregon Pioneer Association; an extremely interesting manuscript journal of Loren L. Williams, covering pioneer life mostly in Oregon, but also in Washington, Idaho, and Montana from 1851-80; many publications of the Oregon Historical Society; and an early magazine, *The Oregon Native Son* (1899-1901). Two newspapers are also part of the collection: *Oregon Herald* (Portland, March 1866-April 1873) and *Oregon Spectator* (Oregon City, February 1846-March 1855).

Bibliographies and Guides

Patricia Brandt and Nancy Guilford. *Oregon Biography Index,* 1976. Indexes forty-seven historical volumes.

Howard McKinley Corning. *Dictionary of Oregon History,* 1956. Covers people, places, events, and organizations. Includes bibliographical references.

Members of the Genealogical Forum of Portland. "Genealogical Research in Oregon." *National Genealogical Society Quarterly* 47 (September 1959): 115-28. Good overview.

Thomas Vaughn and Priscilla Knuth. *A Bibliography of Pacific Northwest History,* 1959. Largely Oregon, very basic.

Periodical and Serial Publications

Klamath Echoes. 16 vols., 1964-78.

Lane County Historian, 1956 to date.

Marion County History. 13 vols., 1955-82.

Oregon Historical Quarterly, 1900 to date.

Overland Journal: Official Journal of the Oregon-California Trails Association, 1983 to date.

Rogue Digger (Rogue Valley Genealogical Society). 10 vols., 1966-75.

UTAH

Researchers will find quite a good collection on Utah and Mormons and Mormonism in Utah at The Newberry Library. Since the Mormons and the history of Utah are so closely intertwined, Mormon historical material relating to Utah is treated in this chapter. Researchers should also see Chapter 10, "Source Material from the Genealogical Department of the Church of Jesus Christ of Latter-day Saints." The

Newberry's Mormon and Mormonism holdings for the entire country are very good and are especially strong for description and travel accounts.

There are good holdings on the State of Deseret (1849-51), including many items on governmental concerns--constitutions, laws, and legislation. One very important source on early Utah is the first thirteen volumes of the *Deseret News*, published in Salt Lake City from June 1850 to September 1864. A short run of *The Mountaineer*, another Salt Lake City newspaper, is available for August 1859 to August 1860. There is also much material on the Utah Expedition of 1857-58. The Newberry's local history holdings are fair to good, and there is some genealogical source material, mostly found in periodicals. One other important source is *Utah: Cities and Towns, 1884-1904*, a microfilm collection of 290 Sanborn maps of twenty-three communities.

Bibliographies and Guides

Chad J. Flake. *A Mormon Bibliography, 1830-1930*, 1978. This volume is not limited to Utah, but has some material of interest. Arrangement is alphabetical by author; there is no subject index.

Laureen Richardson Jaussi and Gloria Duncan Chaston. *Genealogical Records of Utah*, 1974. Very helpful, although the book is largely devoted to governmental and unpublished material. Does include a number of bibliographies of printed material.

Periodical and Serial Publications

Daughters of Utah Pioneers. *Heart Throbs of the West*, 12 vols., 1939-51 and *Our Pioneer Heritage*, 15 vols., 1958-72.

Journal of History. 18 vols., 1908-25. Published by the Reorganized Church of Jesus Christ of Latter Day Saints.

Morgenstjernen (continued as *The Historical Record*). 9 vols., 1882-90. A "monthly periodical, devoted exclusively to historical, biographical, chronological, and statistical matters." Utah and Mormon-related.

Tullidge's Quarterly Magazine, of Utah, her Founders, her Enterprises, and her Civilization. 4 vols., 1880-85.

Utah Genealogical and Historical Magazine. 31 vols., 1910-40. Mormon oriented, published by the Genealogical Society of Utah.

Utah Historical Quarterly, 1928 to date.

Utah, the Mormons and the West, 1969 to date. Series published by the University of Utah Library.

WASHINGTON

Newberry researchers will find much of interest on the State of Washington. There is good material on the fur trade, missions, and on army life and the U. S. military presence. There is also a good collection of description and travel accounts, emigrant guides, and promotional/boosterism literature. The local history collection is good, and some genealogical source material is available, including census indexes, probate records, marriage records, and cemetery transcriptions.

Researchers should be sure to check the Card Catalogue under the headings "Washington (State)" and "Washington (Territory)." Because Washington was first part of Oregon Territory, a search of appropriate Card Catalogue entries under "Oregon" or "Oregon (Territory)" may be advisable.

Two important sources on early Washington are *Washington Territory Donation Land Claims* (1980), compiled by the Seattle Genealogical Society, which contains abstracts of pre-1856 land claims taken from the National Archives records, and the "Isaac Ingalls Stevens Papers, 1831-62," on microfilm from the University of Washington. Stevens was an army officer, governor of Washington Territory, and was involved in the Indian Wars. The library also has the newspaper *Pioneer and Democrat* (formerly *The Columbian*), published at Olympia, for September, 1852 to May, 1861.

Bibliographies and Guides

The Dictionary Catalog of Pacific Northwest Collection of the University of Washington Libraries, Seattle. 6 vols., 1972.

Periodical and Serial Publications

The Big Smoke (Pend Oreille Co.), 1969 to date.

Clark County History, 1960 to date.

Cowlitz County Historical Quarterly, 1959 to date.

Pacific Northwest Quarterly, 1906 to date.

Seattle Genealogical Society Bulletin. Vols. 7-21, 1957-72.

Skamania County Heritage, 1972 to date.

The Sou'wester (Pacific Co.). 14 vols., 1966-79.

Washington Heritage (formerly *Washington State Genealogical and Historical Review*), 1983 to date.

The Washington Historian. 2 vols., 1899-1901.

Publications of the Washington State Historical Society. 3 vols., 1906-40.

CHAPTER 17

FOREIGN SOURCES

CANADA

The Newberry Library's Canadian holdings are quite rich, and one could easily write an extended essay describing them. In this brief chapter, the holdings can only be broadly described and some of the more significant titles mentioned. To identify relevant works in the Card Catalogue, researchers should check the subject headings "Canada," the names of individual provinces, counties and towns, and some additional headings such as "Maritime Provinces," "Canada, Western," "Canada, Northern," and "Northwest, Canadian."

The collection is very good for description and travel literature for all parts of Canada; the map holdings are quite good, although best for national and provincial maps; some directories are available; the Yukon Gold Fields are well covered; and much can be found on the Loyalists in Canada (see Chapter 6 for further information). The local history holdings are fair to good. Regions and counties are better covered than towns, and the collection lacks most pamphlet local histories. The holdings are strongest for the Atlantic Provinces, Ontario, and for recent histories from the Plains Provinces. Researchers will find a great deal of genealogical source material for Nova Scotia, Ontario, and Quebec, including many transcripts of vital records, cemetery transcriptions, vital records from newspapers, probates, and parish registers.

Several organizations and individuals have published vital records from Roman Catholic parish registers, mostly in Quebec Province. The library has actively collected this material and has the volumes published by Jean and Roger Bergeron, Le Centre de Genealogie, Societe Canadienne de Genealogie, Quebec, and others. The library also has many transcripts of the early county marriage records from Ontario Province which begin in 1858.

Some other items of particular interest to local and family historians include two Saskatchewan newspapers on microfilm: *Saskatchewan Herald* (August 1878-December 1900), and *The Prince Albert Times and Saskatchewan Review* (November 1882-December 1895); *Alaska-Yukon Magazine,* 13 volumes (1905-12); many transcriptions and indexes to Canadian censuses, including the 1851 New Brunswick census (the library does not have the Canadian census on microfilm); *Ontario Archives Land Record Index* (1979), which is alphabetical by name of locatee and lists location of land, date of issue, and residence of owner; the very useful series, Ontario Genealogical Society, Ottawa Branch Publications (1973+); and numerous bulletins, reports, and publications from the various provincial archives and the Public Archives of Canada.

The library has Cyprien Tanguay's monumental work on French-Canadian genealogy, *Dictionnaire Genealogique des Familles Canadiennes...* (1871-90), plus the *Complement* (1957-64), a total of ten volumes, covering the years 1608-1763. A recent work which should be used in conjunction with Tanguay is Rene Jette's *Dictionnaire Genealogique des Familles du Quebec* (1983). Jette includes material not found in Tanguay, especially for the period 1621 to 1730.

A great many Canadian historical and genealogical periodicals are found at the library. These include all journals of national scope, all provincial historical journals, but only a few local historical and genealogical periodicals. The library does, however, actively collect publication series from local societies.

The Newberry Library is known for its excellent holdings of bibliographic tools, and the Canadian collection is no exception. Researchers will find a variety of bibliographies, guides, and library catalogues on Canadian provincial and local history and genealogy. Many bibliographical articles have also appeared in Canadian and U. S. historical and genealogical journals. Below is just a *very small* sampling of these bibliographic tools. Researchers should also consult the Canadian section in P. William Filby's *American and British Genealogy and Heraldry,* 3rd edition (1983).

Bibliographies and Guides--Canadian History

A Bibliography of Canadiana. 1 vol. plus supplements, 1934-85. From the collection of the Metropolitan Toronto Library.

J. L. Granatstein and Paul Stevens. *Canada Since 1867: A Bibliographical Guide,* 1974.

The Lawrence Lande Collection of Canadiana in the Redpath Library of

McGill University: A Bibliography..., 1965, plus 1971 supplement.

Catalogue of the Public Archives Library, Public Archives of Canada. 13 vols., 1979.

Dwight L. Smith, ed. *The History of Canada: An Annotated Bibliography*, 1983. Periodical articles taken from *America: History and Life.*

Bibliographies and Guides--Canadian Genealogy
Eunice Ruiter Baker. *Searching for Your Ancestors in Canada,* 1974.

Angus Baxter. *In Search of Your Roots: A Guide for Canadians Seeking their Ancestors,* 1978.

Eric Jonasson. *The Canadian Genealogical Handbook,* 1978.

Public Archives of Canada. *Tracing Your Ancestors in Canada,* updated periodically.

Bibliographies and Guides--Atlantic Provinces
Robert F. Fellows. *Researching Your Ancestors in New Brunswick, Canada,* 1979.

Orlo Jones. *Family History in Prince Edward Island,* 1981.

William F. E. Morley. *Canadian Local Histories to 1850: A Bibliography, The Atlantic Provinces,* 1967.

Terrence Punch. *Genealogical Research in Nova Scotia,* 1978.

Hugh A. Taylor. *New Brunswick History: A Checklist of Secondary Sources,* 1971, plus 1974 supplement.

Bibliographies and Guides--Ontario
Olga B. Bishop. *Bibliography of Ontario History: 1867-1976,* 1980.

Marion C. Keffer, Robert F. Kirk and Audrey L. Kirk. *Some Ontario References and Sources for the Family Historian,* 1976.

William F. E. Morley. *Canadian Local Histories to 1850: A Bibliography, Ontario and the Canadian North,* 1978.

Ontario Historical Studies Series. *Ontario Since 1867: A Bibliography,* 1973.

Bibliographies and Guides--Quebec
Andre Beaulieu and William F. E. Morley. *Canadian Local Histories to 1850: A Bibliography, Province of Quebec,* 1971.

Rene Durocher and Paul-Andre Linteau. *Histoire du Quebec: Bibliographie Selective, (1867-1970),* 1970.

Bibliographies and Guides--Western Provinces

Alan F. Artibise. *Western Canada Since 1870: A Select Bibliography and Guide,* 1978.

Margaret H. Edwards and John C. R. Lort. *A Bibliography of British Columbia: Years of Growth 1900-1950,* 1975.

Gerald Friesen and Barry Potyondi. *A Guide to the Study of Manitoba Local History,* 1981.

Catalogue of the Glenbow Historical Library, Calgary, Canada. 4 vols., 1973.

D'Arcy Hande. *Exploring Family History in Saskatchewan,* 1983.

James R. Lotz. *Yukon Bibliography,* 1964, plus 1973 supplement by C. Anne Hemstock.

Barbara J. Lowther. *A Bibliography of British Columbia,* 1968.

Bruce Braden Peel. *A Bibliography of the Prairie Provinces,* 1973.

Dictionary Catalogue of the Library of the Provincial Archives of British Columbia, Victoria. 8 vols., 1971.

Saskatchewan Archives Board. *Exploring Local History in Saskatchewan,* 1985.

Gloria M. Strathern. *Navigations, Traffiques and Discoveries, 1774-1848,* 1970. On British Columbia.

GREAT BRITAIN

The Newberry Library has an excellent collection of books and manuscripts on England, Scotland, and Wales from the late Middle Ages through the nineteenth century. The collection, which concentrates on history, literature, and religion, is one of the best in the Midwest for sixteenth-, seventeenth-, and eighteenth-century materials. In the field of local and family history, it is one of the best collections in the United States. Researchers will find a wealth of material including many rare and obscure items. This brief chapter can in no way do justice to the scope, size, and range of materials that are available; it can only describe the holdings in general terms and suggest a few bibliographies and guides that will assist researchers.

The Newberry has a superb collection of English and Scottish local histories. These include not only older works, but current publications as well. The library, of course, has *The Victoria History of the Counties of England,* which began publication in 1900 with volume I of Hampshire County. The following bibliographies are useful in identifying local histories.

Local History Bibliographies

John P. Anderson. *The Book of British Topography,* 1881. Lists approximately 14,000 titles from the British Museum Library.

Charles Gross. *A Bibliography of British Municipal History,* 1897, repr. 1966. Very important work.

Geoffrey H. Martin and Sylvia McIntyre. *A Bibliography of British and Irish Municipal History,* 1972. Continues Gross. Very good; includes Wales and Scotland.

The Newberry's holdings of maps, gazetteers, and place name literature for Great Britain are also excellent and are covered in more detail in Chapter 2. Researchers will also find very good holdings of school histories and registers (not just for Oxford and Cambridge), church histories, monumental inscriptions, heraldry and heralds' visitations (see Chapter 7), bibliographies on various aspects of English and Scottish history, and material on the military, including many registers and lists of officers. The Newberry does not have the English census on microfilm, and has only a few census transcriptions and indexes.

The library does have one of the better collections in the United States of English genealogies, although it is not a large collection. It is best for nineteenth- and early twentieth-century publications. The series *Miscellanea Genealogica et Heraldica,* 31 volumes (1868-1938) will also be found at the library. There are several works which will guide researchers to published genealogies, both in book form and as articles in local histories and periodicals.

Guides to Published Genealogies

George W. Marshall. *The Genealogist's Guide.* 4th ed., 1903, reprinted 1967. Lists pedigrees in printed works.

John B. Whitmore. *A Genealogical Guide: An Index to British Pedigrees in Continuation of Marshall's Genealogist's Guide (1903),* 1953.

Geoffrey B. Barrow. *The Genealogist's Guide: An Index to Printed British Pedigrees and Family Histories,* 1977. A supplement to Marshall and Whitmore. For all three of the above guides, the Newberry holdings are excellent for cited local histories and periodicals, but much weaker for book-length family histories.

Cecil R. Humphery-Smith. *A Genealogist's Bibliography.* New ed., 1985. Very good.

Margaret Stuart. *Scottish Family History: A Guide to Works of Reference on the History and Genealogy of Scottish Families,* 1930.

Joan P. S. Ferguson. *Scottish Family History Held in Scottish   Libraries,* 1960. Supplements Stuart.

T. R. Thomson. *A Catalogue of British Family Histories.*   3rd ed. with Addenda, 1980. The library lacks many cited titles. The collection is better for older works.

A great many church histories and parish register publications are available. The library has publications of all parish register societies, as well as the 240 volumes of *Phillimore's Parish Register Series* (1896-1938), which covers approximately 1,400 parishes.   Two works which list parishes and note the location and dates of extant records are *National Index of Parish Registers: A Guide to Anglican, Roman Catholic and Nonconformist Registers Before 1837...* (1967+), edited by Donald J. Steel, and *The Phillimore Atlas and Index of Parish Registers* (1984) by Cecil Humphery-Smith, which contains maps showing pre-1832 parish lines, a list of parishes by county, and notation of extant records. Note is also made of parish records that have been microfilmed by the Latter-day Saints.   Names from many English parish registers have been extracted and added to the International Genealogical Index (IGI) compiled by the LDS Genealogical Department.   Researchers with English ancestry are advised to consult the IGI (see Chapter 10 "Source Material from the Genealogical Department of the Church of Jesus Christ of Latter-day Saints").

Perhaps the greatest strength of the library's local and family history holdings for Great Britain lies in the outstanding collection of serial publications from county and sectional historical societies, national societies, and parish register societies. These include publication series by well-known organizations such as the British Record Society (1888+), Harleian Society (1869+), Scottish Record Society (1898+, volume 1 lacking), Scotland's Spalding Club (1841-1946), and local groups such as the North Riding Record Society (1884-97), the Historical Society of West Wales (1910-29), and the Devon and Cornwall Record Society (1906+).

An excellent guide to these publications is Edward L. C. Mullins' *Texts and Calendars: An Analytical Guide to Serial Publications* (1958, plus 1983 supplement). This work lists serial publications produced by official bodies, such as the Public Record Office, national bodies, English local societies, and Welsh societies.   Local publications of Ireland and Scotland are not included.   The Newberry has over ninety-five percent of all the works listed, including every English local society serial publication, except for two volumes of the Cantilupe Society publications.   A similar work exists for Scotland, although it is not as up-to-date.   Charles S. Terry published *A Catalogue of the Publications of Scottish Historical and Kindred Clubs and Societies...1780-1908* (1909).   Cyril Matheson continued Terry's work with *A Catalogue of the Publications of Scottish Historical and Kindred Clubs and Societies...1908-1927* (1928).

The Newberry collection is very good for historical society publications cited by Terry and Matheson, but lacks many publications of natural history and naturalists clubs.

A very good collection of serial publications from the Public Record Office is available including calendars of Patent Rolls, Close Rolls, Fine Rolls, Inquisitions, Charter Rolls, and calendars of State Papers, both domestic and foreign.

Last, but certainly not least, is the library's very fine collection of English periodicals, many of them quite rare or obscure. These include local history journals and genealogical journals including *Family History News and Digest* (1977+), *The Genealogists' Magazine* (1925+), and the *Scottish Genealogist* (1954+). Also available is a fine collection of eighteenth- and nineteenth-century quarterlies and reviews such as *Gentleman's Magazine* (1731-1907), *Edinburgh Review* (1802-1929), *Blackwood's Edinburgh Magazine* (1817-1971), *Westminster Review* (1824-1914), and many others.

Guides to Genealogical Research

Angus Baxter. *In Search of Your British and Irish Roots,* 1986.

Gerald Hamilton-Edwards. *In Search of British Ancestry.* 3rd ed., 1974.

_____. *In Search of Scottish Ancestry,* 1973.

_____. *In Search of Welsh Ancestry,* 1985.

Alwyn James. *Scottish Roots,* 1981.

Anthony R. Wagner. *English Genealogy.* 3rd ed., 1983.

IRELAND

This chapter deals exclusively with the local history and genealogy of Ireland, not with the general history of Ireland, nor the Irish in America. Related material will be found in Chapter 5 "Ethnic and Native American Sources," and Chapter 8 "Passenger Lists and Naturalization Records." Despite the dire pronouncements of some that "all Irish records were lost in 1922 in the Public Record Office of Ireland fire," the serious researcher knows this is not true. The Newberry has an excellent collection of historical material on Ireland from the late Middle Ages through the nineteenth century, including one of the finest collections on Irish local and family history in the country. The Newberry is one of the few places where all the major research tools, plus extensive supporting material, will be found.

One of the major research tools is Sir Richard Griffith's *General Valuation of Rateable Property in Ireland, 1848-1864.* This listing of property values, done to assess taxes for poor relief, has names of tenants, their lessors, descriptions of property and its value. Griffith's

Valuation, along with the *Index of Surnames of Householders in Griffith's Valuation and Tithe Applotment Books* (1978), is available on microfiche.

Another source that complements Griffith's *Valuation* is the Newberry's complete set of the Ordnance Survey Townland Maps for Ireland. These maps, which represent some of the finest examples of copper engraving known, are on a scale of six inches to the mile, and are based on surveys taken between 1829 and 1842. The last volume was published in 1846. Copies of these maps can be made for library patrons from the Newberry's full-frame microfiche set of the Ordnance Survey Maps. Griffith's *Valuation* and the Ordnance Survey Maps can be used together; references in the *Valuation* refer to specific plates of the maps. The library also has the published volumes of the surveyor's field notes for twenty-nine counties, edited by Michael O'Flanagan. The works listed above are only a few of the highlights in a very good collection of Irish geographical sources found at the library, including maps, atlases, gazetteers, and place name guides such as *A Topographical Dictionary of Ireland,* 2 volumes plus atlas (1837) by Samuel Lewis and *General Alphabetical Index of the Townlands and Towns, Parishes, and Baronies of Ireland Based on the Census of Ireland for the Year 1851* (1861, reprinted 1984).

The collection of Irish local histories is very good to excellent. A large number of gravestone inscriptions are available, both those that have appeared in journals and those published separately. A small collection of Irish family genealogies is part of the holdings. Good material can also be found on Irish emigration.

Below are listed some of the general Irish historical and genealogical journals, but the Newberry also has a number of local historical journals. These range from better known journals such as the *Cork Historical and Archaeological Society Journal* (1892+), to *North Munster Antiquarian Journal* (1936+), *Galway Archaeological and Historical Journal* (1900+), the *Clogher Record* (1967+) and more.

Several other works deserve special mention. Rosemary Folliott has compiled *Index to Biographical Notices in the Newspapers of Limerick, Ennis, Clonmel, and Waterford, 1758-1821* (1985), and *Biographical Notices (Primarily Relating to Counties Cork and Kerry) Collected from Newspapers, 1756-1827, With a Few References, 1749-1755* (1969). Albert E. Casey's and Thomas E. Dowling's *O'Kief, Coshe, Mang, Slieve Lougher, and Upper Blackwater in Ireland,* 15 volumes (1952-71), contains abstracts of records and reproductions of some books relating to the counties of Cork and Kerry. Finally, the Newberry does have many volumes of the Irish almanac and directory, *Thom's Official Directory of Ireland.* The library's holdings are spotty from 1846 to 1888, but nearly complete from 1889-1958.

Bibliographies and Guides

Donal F. Begley, ed. *Irish Genealogy: A Record Finder,* 1981. Very good. Lists gravestone inscriptions in printed sources.

Brian de Breffny. *Bibliography of Irish Family History and Genealogy,* 1974.

Alan R. Eager. *A Guide to Irish Bibliographical Material: A Bibliography of Irish Bibliographies and Sources of Information.* 2nd ed., 1980. Very good.

Margaret Dickson Falley. *Irish and Scotch-Irish Ancestral Research.* 2 vols, 1961-62. Excellent, essential work. Bibliographies in volume 2 are very useful.

The Genealogical Department of the Church of Jesus Christ of Latter-day Saints. *Basic Genealogical Research Guide for Ireland.* Research Paper Series A, No. 58, 1978.

Charles Gross. *A Bibliography of British Municipal History,* 1897, repr. 1966. Very good.

Geoffrey H. Martin and Sylvia McIntyre. *A Bibliography of British and Irish Municipal History,* 1972. Continues Gross. Very good.

Sources for the History of Irish Civilization. 9 vols., 1970. Covers articles published in over 150 Irish periodicals between 1800 and 1969.

Periodical and Serial Publications

All-Ireland Heritage, 1984 to date.

Analecta Hibernica (Irish Manuscripts Commission), 1930 to date.

Richard S. J. Clarke. *Gravestone Inscriptions, County Down.* 19 vols., 1966-81.

Cork Historical and Archaeological Society Journal, 1892 to date.

Dublin Historical Record, 1938 to date.

The Irish Ancestor, 1969 to date.

The Irish Genealogist, 1937 to date.

Irish Historical Studies, 1938 to date.

Journal of the Irish Memorials Association. 13 vols. (Newberry lacks vols. 10 and 11), 1888/91-1933/37.

Parish Register Society of Dublin. 12 vols., 1906-15.

Report of the Deputy Keeper of the Public Records of Ireland, 1869 to date.

Report of the Deputy Keeper of the Records (Northern Ireland), 1924 to date.

GERMANY

Because so many family historians have Germanic roots, this chapter on Germany is included, although the Newberry does not have a particularly distinguished Germanic collection. This chapter deals specifically with Newberry sources relevant to Germanic genealogy, not with German history nor German-Americans. Related material is found in Chapter 5 "Ethnic and Native American Sources," Chapter 8 "Passenger Lists and Naturalization Records," Chapter 7 "Heraldry, Nobility, and Heriditary Socities," and Chapter 2 "Maps, Atlases and Geographical Sources."

The library collects works on Germany from the late Middle Ages to the end of the Napoleonic era, although the collection is spotty in places even within those confines. The collection is quite strong for the Middle Ages and Renaissance. The Newberry also has a very fine collection on German heraldry and royal and noble families, which includes many early, rare works. Very little local history, especially for cities and towns, will be found. And, many of the local histories in the collection do not deal with the nineteenth and twentieth centuries, which are of most interest to genealogists. Most of the books cited in this chapter are in German.

The Newberry is one of the few libraries in the United States to have the set *Americana in Deutschen Sammlungen* (Americana in German Collections), 6 volumes (1967), an inventory of material on United States history held by archives and libraries in the Federal Republic of Germany and West Berlin. *ADS* does not contain transcripts of the actual material itself. In most cases, a researcher finding something of interest in *ADS* will need to contact the library or archive in Germany for additional information.

One of the most important sources for German genealogy is the *Deutsches Geschlechterbuch* (German Genealogy or Family Book) (1889+), a series of collected genealogies, now approaching 200 volumes. Some volumes cover geographical areas, while others are of a general nature. Most families included in this work are well-to-do members of the upper middle class and nobility. There is a cumulated index (not every name) to the first 150 volumes.

The Newberry holds some material on German emigration, both in the form of emigration studies and emigrant lists. The library does not, however, have the Hamburg Departure Lists. For lists of emigrants, researchers should especially see Clifford Neal Smith's German-American Genealogical Research Monograph Series (1973+) and German and Central European Emigration Monograph Series (1980+); *The Wuerttemberg Emigration Index* (1986+) by Trudy Schenk and Ruth

Froelke; and Wilhelm Iwan's *Die Altlutherische Auswanderung um die Mitte des 19. Jahrhunderts* (Old Lutheran Emigration around the Middle of the Nineteenth Century) (1943). Also available are a number of works on die Leichenpredigten (funeral sermons). These include both catalogues and abstracts of the funeral sermons, which were printed and distributed from the mid-sixteenth century through the eighteenth century. Most of the sermons are for upper class Lutherans.

Bibliographies and Guides (in English)

Arbeitsgemeinschaft Ostdeutscher Familienforscher, ed. *Genealogical Guide to German Ancestors from East Germany and Eastern Europe,* 1984. Good.

Virginia Eschenbach. *Searching for Your German Ancestors,* 1976. Brief, but useful.

Charles M. Hall. *The Atlantic Bridge to Germany.* 5 vols. to date, 1974+. Very good guide to records and sources. Includes some helpful maps.

Larry O. Jensen. *A Genealogical Handbook of German Research.* Rev. ed., 1978.

J. Konrad. *German Family Research Made Simple.* 2nd ed., 1977.

Clifford Neal Smith and Anna Piszczan-Czaja Smith. *American Genealogical Resources in German Archives,* 1977. Contains a partial index to *ADS* by surname, geographical area, and subject.

Clifford Neal Smith. *Encyclopedia of German-American Genealogical Research,* 1976. Contains a section on genealogical research in Germany.

Maralyn A. Wellauer. *Tracing Your German Roots,* 1978.

Bibliographies and Guides (in German)

Friedrich Christoph Georg Dahlmann-Waitz. *Dahlmann-Waitz: Quellenkunde der Deutschen Geschichte* (Sources of Information on German History). New ed., 1965+. The standard bibliography of German history. The first edition was published in two volumes, 1931-32.

Rudolf A. Dimpfel. *Biographische Nachschlagewerke, Adelslexika, Wappenbücher; Systematische Zusammenstellung für Historiker und Genealogen* (Biographical Reference Works: Lexica of the Nobility and Books on Heraldry, Systematically Arranged for Historians and Genealogists), 1922. Important bibliographical reference work.

Familiengeschichtliche Bibliographie (Family History Bibliography), 1900+. The Newberry has volumes 1-7, 11 and 16, covering the years 1900-45, 1960-62, and 1975-77. Volumes 12-15 have not yet been published.

Eckhart Henning and Wolfgang Ribbe. *Handbuch der Genealogie* (Handbook of Genealogy), 1972. Very good.

_____. *Taschenbuch für Familiengeschichtsforschung* (Pocketbook for Family History Research). 9th ed., 1980. Good.

Eduard Heydenreich. *Handbuch der Praktischen Genealogie* (Handbook of Practical Genealogy). 2nd ed., 1913, reprinted 1971.

Erich Keyser. *Bibliographie zur Städtegeschichte Deutschlands* (Bibliography of German Town Histories), 1969. Good.

Erich Wentscher and Hermann Mitgau. *Einführung in die Praktische Genealogie* (Introduction to Practical Genealogy), 1966.

Collective Works on German Genealogy and the Nobility

Genealogisches Handbuch des Adels (Genealogical Handbook of the Nobility), 1951+. Continues much of the information in the *Almanach de Gotha (1764-1944)*.

Genealogisches Taschenbuch der Adeligen Häuser (Genealogical Pocketbook of the Noble Houses). Vols. 14-19, 1889-94.

Gothaischer Genealogischer Hofkalender (Genealogical Court Calendar). 17 scattered vols., 1797, 1818, 1871-1907.

Gothaisches Genealogisches Taschenbuch der Adeligen Häuser (Genealogical Pocketbook of the Noble Houses). 38 vols., 1900-39.

Gothaisches Genealogisches Taschenbuch der Freiherrlichen Häuser (Genealogical Pocketbook of the Baronial Houses). Vols. 39-89, and 92, 1889-1939, 1942.

Gothaisches Genealogisches Taschenbuch der Gräflichen Häuser (Genealogical Pocketbook of the Houses of Counts). Vols. 62-112, 1889-1939.

Periodical and Serial Publications

Archiv für Sippenforschung und Alle Verwandten Gebiete (Archive for Genealogical Research and all Related Fields). 20 vols., 1924-43.

Archiv für Stamm- und Wappenkunde (Archive for Family and Heraldic Research). 20 vols., 1900-20.

Blätter des Bayerischen Landesverein für Familienkunde (Papers of the Bavarian Society for Family Research), 1923 to date.

Familiengeschichtliche Quellen (Family History Sources). 13 vols., 1926-59.

Genealogie: Deutsche Zeitschrift für Familienkunde (Genealogy: German Journal for Family Research), 1952 to date. Formerly *Familie und Volk.*

Germanic Genealogist, 1974 to date.

Der Schlüssel (The Key), 1950 to date. Indexes German genealogical periodicals.

INDEX

records of the U.S. District Court for the District of Columbia relating to slaves, 91

Door County Historical Society, Wis., 141

Down County, Ireland, 181

Draper, Lyman C. Manuscripts, 71-72, 111, 119, 121

Dublin, Ireland, 181

Duke of York Record, 90

Dutch-Americans, 33-34, 36, 58

Dutchess County, N.Y., 98

E

East Tennessee Land Company, 119

Eastern Nebraska Genealogical Society, 152

El Paso County, Tex., 156

Emigrant guides, 34

England. *See* Great Britain

English Surnames Series, 19

Ennis, Ireland, 180

Episcopal Church, 117, 145 (*See also* Protestant Episcopal Church and Methodist Episcopal Church)

Erie County, N.Y., 98

Ethnic sources, 9, 21, 33-36 (*See also* names of ethnic groups)

Evangelical Lutheran Church of St. Luke, Chicago, 31, 129

Evan's Early American Imprints. *See* Readex

Evanston, Ill., 11, 129

Everett, Robert, family, 6

F

Fairfax County, Va., 91

Family associations, 54

Family newsletters, 9

Far West, 159-71

Fargo, N. Dak., 11, 136, 146, 147

Faulkner County, Ark., 107

Fayette County, Pa., 99

Federal Writers' Project, 20, 21, 148

First Presbyterian Church of Wheaton, Illinois, 30, 31, 129

Five Civilized Tribes, 37, 38

Flentye, Henry, 6

Florida, 18, 107-08
    census schedules, state and territorial, 27-28, 107

Florida State Historical Society, 108

Florida State University studies, 107

Florida, west, 105, 108

Fort Wayne, Ind., 11, 132

France, 9, 20, 24, 43, 51-52, 54, 74

Franklin, Pa., 101

Franklin (State), 119

Fredericktown, Mo., 31

Freedmen's Bureau, 34

Freedmen's Bureau Field Office records, 91, 104, 114, 155

Freedmen's Saving and Trust Company, 34

Freedmen's Savings and Trust Company, Indexes to Deposit Ledgers, 1865-1874, 104

Freedman's Savings and Trust Company registers, 1865-1874, 104

French-Americans, 33, 118

French in Illinois, 127

O

P

Series, 55
Society of Friends. *See* Quakers
Society of Indiana Pioneers, 56,
131
Society of Montana Pioneers, 151
Sons of the American Revolu-
tion, 55
Soundex, 25-26
South, the, 42, 103-105
South Carolina, 6, 42, 108-09, 117-
18
South Carolina Historical Com-
mission, 117
South Dakota, 23, 24, 146 (*See
also* Dakotas)
South Dakota Historical Society,
147
South Hempstead, N.Y., 95
South Platte Land Company, 68
South Suburban Genealogical
and Historical Society, Ill.,
130
Southeast Texas Genealogical
and Historical Society, 156
Southern California Historical
Society. *See* Historical
Society of Southern California
Southern Land and Investment
Company (Iowa), 69
Southwestern Oklahoma Histori-
cal Society, 154
Spalding Club, 178
Spain, 20, 24, 51, 53-54
Spain in America, 107-08, 112-13,
120, 137, 149, 152, 154, 162-63
Sparta and Elba Land Office,
Ala., 106
Spencer, Platt Rogers, 6
Springfield, Mass., 6
Stamford, Connecticut, Town
Meeting Records, 77
State Census Schedules. *See*

Census
State Historical Society of Wis-
consin, 140
State Library of Ohio, the, 139
Steamship directories, 58
Stebbins family, 12
Sterling, Ill., 128
Steubenville, Ohio, 139
Stevens, Isaac Ingalls, Papers,
1831-1864, 170
Stockton Corral of the
Westerners, 165
Strang, James Jesse, 134
Surnames, 19-20
Sweden, 24, 53
Swedish-Americans, 34, 58
Switzerland, 53
Syracuse, N.Y., 12

T

Tallahassee Historical Society,
Fla., 108
Taylor, R.J., Foundation, 109
Telephone books, 10, 129
Tennessee, 11, 21, 119-20
Tennessee County History Series,
119
Territorial census schedules. *See*
Census
Texas, 24, 33, 45, 154-56
Texas Association, 154
Texas Genealogical Society, 156
Texas, University of, 155,
Toledo, Ohio, 12
Topsfield, Mass., 82
Tucson Corral of the Westerners,
163
Tuolumne County, Calif., 165